Issues in Pricing Undergraduate Education

Larry H. Litten, *Editor*

NEW DIRECTIONS FOR INSTITUTIONAL RESEARCH
Sponsored by the Association for Institutional Research
MARVIN W. PETERSON, PATRICK T. TERENZINI
Editors-in-Chief

Number 42, June 1984

Paperback sourcebooks in
The Jossey-Bass Higher Education Series

Jossey-Bass Inc., Publishers
San Francisco • Washington • London

Larry H. Litten (Ed.).
Issues in Pricing Undergraduate Education.
New Directions for Institutional Research, no. 42.
Volume XI, number 2.
San Francisco: Jossey-Bass, 1984

New Directions for Institutional Research Series
Marvin W. Peterson, Patrick T. Terenzini, *Editors-in-Chief*

Copyright © 1984 by Jossey-Bass Inc., Publishers
and
Jossey-Bass Limited

Copyright under International, Pan American, and Universal Copyright Conventions. All rights reserved. No part of this issue may be reproduced in any form—except for brief quotation (not to exceed 500 words) in a review or professional work—without permission in writing from the publishers.

New Directions for Institutional Research (publication number USPS 098-830) is published quarterly by Jossey-Bass Inc., Publishers, and is sponsored by the Association for Institutional Research. The volume and issue numbers above are included for the convenience of libraries. Second-class postage rates paid at San Francisco, California, and at additional mailing offices.

Correspondence:
Subscriptions, single-issue orders, change of address notices, undelivered copies, and other correspondence should be sent to Subscriptions, Jossey-Bass Inc., Publishers, 433 California Street, San Francisco California 94104.

Editorial correspondence should be sent to the Editor-in-Chief, Marvin W. Peterson, Center for the Study of Higher Education, University of Michigan, Ann Arbor, Michigan 48109, or Patrick T. Terenzini, Office of Institutional Research, SUNY, Albany, New York 12222.

Library of Congress Catalogue Card Number LC 83-82728
International Standard Serial Number ISSN 0271-0560
International Standard Book Number ISBN 87589-775-4

Cover art by Willi Baum
Manufactured in the United States of America

Ordering Information

The paperback sourcebooks listed below are published quarterly and can be ordered either by subscription or single-copy.

Subscriptions cost $35.00 per year for institutions, agencies, and libraries. Individuals can subscribe at the special rate of $25.00 per year *if payment is by personal check.* (Note that the full rate of $35.00 applies if payment is by institutional check, even if the subscription is designated for an individual.) Standing orders are accepted. Subscriptions normally begin with the first of the four sourcebooks in the current publication year of the series. When ordering, please indicate if you prefer your subscription to begin with the first issue of the *coming* year.

Single copies are available at $8.95 when payment accompanies order, and *all single-copy orders under $25.00 must include payment.* (California, New Jersey, New York, and Washington, D.C., residents please include appropriate sales tax.) For billed orders, cost per copy is $8.95 plus postage and handling. (Prices subject to change without notice.)

Bulk orders (ten or more copies) of any individual sourcebook are available at the following discounted prices: 10–49 copies, $8.05 each; 50–100 copies, $7.15 each; over 100 copies, *inquire.* Sales tax and postage and handling charges apply as for single copy orders.

To ensure correct and prompt delivery, all orders must give either the *name of an individual* or an *official purchase order number.* Please submit your order as follows:

Subscriptions: specify series and year subscription is to begin.
Single Copies: specify sourcebook code (such as, IR8) and first two words of title.

Mail orders for United States and Possessions, Latin America, Canada, Japan, Australia, and New Zealand to:
  Jossey-Bass Inc., Publishers
  433 California Street
  San Francisco, California 94104

Mail orders for all other parts of the world to:
  Jossey-Bass Limited
  28 Banner Street
  London EC1Y 8QE

New Directions for Institutional Research Series
Marvin W. Peterson, Patrick T. Terenzini
Editors-in-Chief

IR1 *Evaluating Institutions for Accountability,* Howard R. Bowen
IR2 *Assessing Faculty Effort,* James I. Doi
IR3 *Toward Affirmative Action,* Lucy W. Sells
IR4 *Organizing Nontraditional Study,* Samuel Baskin

IR5   *Evaluating Statewide Boards,* Robert O. Berdahl
IR6   *Assuring Academic Progress Without Growth,* Allan M. Cartter
IR7   *Responding to Changing Human Resource Needs,* Paul Heist, Jonathan R. Warren
IR8   *Measuring and Increasing Academic Productivity,* Robert A. Wallhaus
IR9   *Assessing Computer-Based System Models,* Thomas R. Mason
IR10 *Examining Departmental Management,* James Smart, James Montgomery
IR11 *Allocating Resources Among Departments,* Paul L. Dressel, Lou Anna Kimsey Simon
IR12 *Benefiting from Interinstitutional Research,* Marvin W. Peterson
IR13 *Applying Analytic Methods to Planning and Management,* David S. P. Hopkins, Roger G. Schroeder
IR14 *Protecting Individual Rights to Privacy in Higher Education,* Alton L. Taylor
IR15 *Appraising Information Needs of Decision Makers,* Carl R. Adams
IR16 *Increasing the Public Accountability of Higher Education,* John K. Folger
IR17 *Analyzing and Constructing Cost,* Meredith A. Gonyea
IR18 *Employing Part-Time Faculty,* David W. Leslie
IR19 *Using Goals in Research and Planning,* Robert Fenske
IR20 *Evaluating Faculty Performance and Vitality,* Wayne C. Kirschling
IR21 *Developing a Total Marketing Plan,* John A. Lucas
IR22 *Examining New Trends in Administrative Computing,* E. Michael Staman
IR23 *Professional Development for Institutional Research,* Robert G. Cope
IR24 *Planning Rational Retrenchment,* Alfred L. Cooke
IR25 *The Impact of Student Financial Aid on Institutions,* Joe B. Henry
IR26 *The Autonomy of Public Colleges,* Paul L. Dressel
IR27 *Academic Program Evaluation,* Eugene C. Craven
IR28 *Academic Planning for the 1980s,* Richard B. Heydinger
IR29 *Institutional Assessment for Self-Improvement,* Richard I. Miller
IR30 *Coping with Faculty Reduction,* Stephen R. Hample
IR31 *Evaluation of Management and Planning Systems,* Nick L. Poulton
IR32 *Increasing the Use of Program Evaluation,* Jack Lindquist
IR33 *Effective Planned Change Strategies,* G. Melvin Hipps
IR34 *Qualitative Methods for Institutional Research,* Eileen Kuhns, S. V. Martorana
IR35 *Information Technology: Advances and Applications,* Bernard Sheehan
IR36 *Studying Student Attrition,* Ernest T. Pascarella
IR37 *Using Research for Strategic Planning,* Norman P. Uhl
IR38 *The Politics and Pragmatics of Institutional Research,* James W. Firnberg, William F. Lasher
IR39 *Applying Methods and Techniques of Futures Research,* James L. Morrison, William L. Renfro, Wayne I. Boucher
IR40 *College Faculty: Versatile Human Resources in a Period of Constraint,* Roger G. Baldwin, Robert T. Blackburn
IR41 *Determining the Effectiveness of Campus Services,* Robert A. Scott

Contents

Editor's Notes 1
Larry H. Litten
A variety of disciplinary and organizational perspectives is required when dealing with pricing issues in higher education. Although pricing is a central and universal concern in social organizations, some particular characteristics of higher education affect the nature of prices associated with an undergraduate education.

Chapter 1. Perspectives on Pricing 7
Susan Shaman, Robert M. Zemsky
A conceptual framework helps in sorting through the complex issues of pricing by distinguishing among different types of monetary prices and different pricing strategies.

Chapter 2. Using Enrollment Demand Models in Institutional Pricing Decisions 19
William C. Weiler
A planner shows how institutional pricing decisions can benefit from the use of enrollment demand models that help identify the enrollment and fiscal effects of differentiated tuitions based on program costs.

Chapter 3. Priorities, Planning, and Prices 35
Timothy Warner
A university budget officer examines undergraduate tuition in the broader context of institutional costs and prices, and discusses the financial and administrative implications of various pricing strategies.

Chapter 4. The Politics and Practicalities of Pricing in Academe 47
Joseph E. Gilmour, Jr., J. Lloyd Suttle
Two case studies—Yale University and the State of Washington—explore the political aspects of price setting in a private institution and a public higher education system.

Chapter 5. Reducing the Burden of Price 63
Janet S. Hansen
Discounts, credit, subsidized employment, and tax policy are discussed as devices for reducing the burden that financial prices impose on educational consumers and on the people who help pay their bills.

Chapter 6. Pricing in Higher Education: A Marketing Perspective 77
Patrick E. Murphy
A marketer considers both financial and nonfinancial costs of education as influences on consumer behavior and as elements that an institution can manage in its efforts to maintain or change its position in the market.

Chapter 7. Advancing the Research Agenda on Undergraduate Pricing 91
Larry H. Litten

The complex issues concerning pricing an undergraduate education require further research; the principal research questions and some relevant readings and other resources are listed in this chapter.

Index 99

Editor's Notes

The prices of goods and services have a pronounced and pervasive influence on the lives of individuals and the existence of organizations. The prices that an organization sets for its goods or services inform consumers how much of their personal resources they must part with in order to obtain the benefits that they desire from these goods and services. Thus, prices affect consumers' decisions to purchase a good or service and their choices of suppliers. For organizations, prices influence their incomes both by affecting the level of demand for their products and by determining the amount of money that flows from each unit of a good or service that is delivered. Thus, price is a key link between the parties in a market—producers and consumers—and it is a major governor of behavior and the movement of resources.

The prices that organizations place on their goods and services influence the general structure of the market and the current well-being (wealth or benefits enjoyed) of individuals and organizations. Prices are also a key element in the planning that both individuals and organizations do for the future. All organizations have to consider the prices that they pay for the resources that they need and the prices that they charge for the goods and and services that they provide. Institutions of higher education are no exception to this rule.

Colleges and universities enjoy various kinds of contributed income, principally from public subsidies and private philanthropy. However, much of their income is earned, especially for institutions in the independent sector. Earned income comes as direct payment for services rendered at prices set or negotiated by the institution or by the agency that controls it. While research contracts and sales of tickets, journals, and books all generate earned income for colleges and universities, the principal source of earned income is the tuition, fees, and room and board charges that students pay for educational services—instruction, certification, socialization, and the sustenance, social, cultural, and recreational offerings associated with college life. This *New Directions* sourcebook focuses on the prices set for educational services in this broad sense at the undergraduate level.

Prices exist at the interface between the demand and the supply sides of a market. It is impossible to consider issues of price fully without dealing with the perspectives both of the consumers who pay the prices and of the organizations that set the prices. The authors of the chapters that follow deal both with the setting of prices—how, by whom, for what, and so on—and with the effects that prices can have.

With annual comprehensive fees at some independent institutions now well into the five-digit range and with the doubling of student charges in both the public and the independent sectors over the past decade (Hartle and Wabnick, 1983), college and university prices have captured the attention of politicians, business and civic leaders, the media, and the general public. With reports that the average total student charges for a year of traditional undergraduate education in an independent institution represent more than 100 percent of the median discretionary family income and that college costs have begun to rise faster than family incomes (Hartle and Wabnick, 1983), concern is escalating. There are wide variations in published prices across institutions, ranging from no tuition to almost $3,000 for in-state students in public institutions and from less than $2,000 to almost $10,000 in the independent sector. These figures conceal some exceptional conditions that introduce additional variation within the independent sector. For example, Berea College, with its extensive work program, has no tuition, while many independent institutions have only a comprehensive fee that includes tuition, room, and board that is considerably above the $10,000 mark. These variations, which are compounded by elaborate discounting systems that create an entirely different distribution of net prices, are confusing to laymen. For all these reasons, the subject of prices in higher education has engendered both interest and alarm.

Morgan (1983) has suggested that higher education may well be following the path of the health care industry in America, with which it shares some striking characteristics. The public and its political representatives have shifted their concerns about health care from access to cost—or more precisely, to price—containment. Morgan predicts that a variety of control mechanisms may emerge in higher education—formal planning and coordination requirements, direct government regulation, and enhanced market mechanisms—following the patterns observed in the health care industry.

The specific issues of how prices are set, the goods or services that they cover, and their effects on consumer and organizational behavior and well-being have intrinsic interest for students of organizations, and they have great practical import for managers of organizations. In an era of potentially shrinking demand for higher education, the interest in pricing increases. To what extent can the negative effects of demographic shifts be offset by charging a higher per-unit price for services rendered? This question has particular interest for organizations such as colleges and universities that have relatively inflexible production resources (for example, relatively unconvertible physical plants, campuses, and instructional laboratory equipment, and highly specialized, tenured faculty). As nontuition sources of earned income, such as contract research for the government, also decrease the issue of income that can be raised from the declining pool of students becomes even more urgent. However, it is difficult both to set prices and to predict their effects in an economy in which various indicators of national economic capacity or well-being—per capita income, inflation, productivity—seem to be moving in inconsistent directions.

The demonstrated and presumed effects of price levels on students' participation in higher education and on students' choices of colleges signal the importance of price to analysts of higher education and to the administrators and trustees of its institutions. Although other industries provide some provocative evidence (Gale and Klavens, 1983) that price reductions result in market share increases that are much shorter-lived than improvements in product quality or benefits delivered to consumers (because competitors can more readily match price reductions than quality enhancements), we can expect considerable maneuvering on the pricing front in higher education. Extensive price discounting schemes (especially merit or nonneed aid), which some consider the harbinger of a price war (Deitch, 1981), have already caught the attention of the public and professionals.

Several characteristics of higher education complicate the pricing issues that colleges and universities face. Higher education is a nonprofit activity. As such, its pricing objectives often differ substantially from those of organizations in the profit-making sector. Higher education is essentially a service activity. Marketing theorists have identified several properties that make the marketing of services different from the marketing of goods. The most important is that the consumer is directly involved in the production process for many services. That is, services are not simply manufactured by the selling organization; many services are created through interaction between and efforts by both the supplier and the consumer. Education is a prime example of such a service: Learning cannot take place unless the student is willing to expend some time and effort. This means that the consumer must bear substantial nonfinancial costs to participate in educational activities. These nonfinancial costs become part of the total price of the educational experience. An institution can manage—that is, alter—these costs to improve its market position.

Students do more than produce private benefits through their personal educational efforts; they also help to create the educational environment of an institution, and they are factors in the production of benefits for other students. At many institutions, some types of students—for example, very intelligent students and students with exceptional athletic or other extracurricular skills—are believed to contribute more to the institution's quality than others do. In some instances, such students can in turn exact a price from the institution for matriculating. Most frequently, this prices comes as a reduction in the financial price that the institution charges for the educational services that it provides. This reduction can take the form of a scholarship, favorable credit, or employment opportunities. Institution building through selective price discounting appears to be on the rise. Such discounting has occurred at a highly targeted level that would not be tolerated in other parts of the economy because it has developed at a margin of a generally accepted system for subsidizing through financial aid the public benefits of higher education.

Higher education is a complex set of functions. Undergraduate education is only one part of the enterprise. Joint production functions across several areas—instruction and research, graduate and undergraduate instruction—and joint costs across production areas greatly complicate cost analysis and pricing. Even undergraduate education involves a complex array of benefits and ways to achieve those benefits. Education in a college setting is an investment whose benefits to the consumer are generally realized over time. In many institutions, there is also a large consumption component to the undergraduate experience—the immediate rewards of living in a college environment. The price of a college education thus involves a number of long-and short-term benefits from the consumer's point of view and a wide variety of services from the institution's point of view. Payment of the major part of the nonfinancial price extends over a minimum of four years for the traditional bachelor's degree, and payment of the financial price often extends well beyond graduation when credit is involved. This extended purchase period also means that forgone income is a very large component of the total price of a college education. Thus, from any perspective, undergraduate education involves a complex price, or set of prices.

The dollars charged for various services and the time and effort required to prepare for and complete individual courses and entire programs can all be manipulated by an institution in its price setting. In principle, the complexity of higher education prices should create wide latitude for institutions in developing their prices. In reality, this very complexity can inhibit pricing innovations by inducing conservatism among consumers. The complexity of both product and price in higher education creates a substantial set of research issues. How do consumers of educational services use prices, and what effects do prices have on consumers?

The complexity of the services that colleges and universities offer and of the prices that they set for them is compounded for the analyst of higher education pricing by a correspondingly complex set of price payers. The most immediate beneficiary of the educational purchase, the student, generally pays only a small portion of the financial price of education but the largest portion of the nonfinancial price and of the income forgone. It is difficult to find a more elaborate system of second- and third-party payers in our economy. Parents pay a major portion of the direct financial price, governments (and the taxpayers who support them) subsidize large amounts of the price through a variety of mechanisms, and institutions allocate some of the costs to donors and to other sources of revenue. Employers of graduates pay indirectly through general taxes, philanthropy, and higher wages to degree recipients, which encourage up-front private and public investments. Again, the potential for variation and innovation in setting prices and determining who pays for what is enormous, and the related set of research issues is equally great.

This sourcebook is concerned principally with the research agenda for pricing issues in higher education. To help readers to take their bearings on this agenda, the contributors draw on their professional experience, theory, and research that relate to these issues. They note a number of recent developments in the pricing and financing of undergraduate education that have been implemented in institutions of higher education and at the federal level. Much ferment is evident in these areas, and there is promise of even more activity to come. Considerable research remains to be done to evaluate the effects of current and emerging practices in higher education pricing. Further research should provide insights that can lead to additional initiatives in setting prices and creating innovative payment mechanisms. This volume should help to clarify the agenda for researchers as well as to provoke the thinking of administrators who have responsibility for developing and implementing policies in these areas.

The central role played by prices in influencing demand and in generating and allocating resources means that prices touch every constituency in an eduational organization and its markets. As multifaceted symbols and behavior-influencing mechanisms, prices must be studied from a variety of perspectives within and across institutions. The chapters of this volume capture just such an array of perspectives by representing the views of faculty, academic staff, and line administrators; of administrators from the budgeting, academic, chief executive officer's, and planning areas; and of institutional and associational personnel. Different intellectual disciplines—economics, sociology, psychology, marketing, history—each provide useful perspectives. Again, the authors draw on several of these disciplines.

In Chapter One, Susan Shaman, a statistician, and Robert Zemsky, an historian turned planner, set the stage for a consideration of pricing issues by presenting some historical observations, a conceptual framework for pricing principles, and a discussion of pricing issues as observed from the Office of Planning Analysis at the University of Pennsylvania. In Chapter Two, William Weiler, an economist, presents an analytical model that relates enrollment demand and pricing, and he examines a number of important considerations to be attended to when developing such a model. Weiler's work illustrates the approaches used in the Office of Management Planning and Information Services at the University of Minnesota.

In Chapter Three, Timothy Warner provides the budget officer's perspective by focusing on the relationships between tuition prices and a university's other sources of income and expenses. Writing from the vantage point of the Office of Management and Budget in the Stanford University Provost's Office, he discusses the administrative implications of various pricing policies. In Chapter Four, Joseph (Tim) Gilmour, Jr., and Lloyd Suttle, both organizational behavior specialists, adopt a political perspective to discuss the various interest groups and processes that affect price setting. These authors use case studies drawn from their experiences in the public and independent sectors to explore the establishment of tuition levels in the State of Washington and at Yale University.

In Chapter Five, Janet Hansen, a public policy analyst, brings a close association with the federal financial aid scene gained from her work at the Washington office of The College Board to her discussion of how students and their families can handle the financial prices attached to an undergraduate degree. She focuses on means that are already in place and on proposals that are now being considered for reducing the burden that these prices represent. In Chapter Six, Patrick Murphy, a professor of marketing, contributes the broad perspective of marketing on prices. Not only are there financial prices, but higher education requires a host of nonfinancial resources from consumers, and it involves a number of risks as well. Colleges and universities can influence their relationships with their markets by managing this entire array of prices. Finally, Chapter Seven lists research questions related to the pricing of undergraduate education and provides a bibliography of relevant resources.

Larry H. Litten
Editor

References

Deitch, K. M. "A Price War for Higher Education." *Change,* 1981, *13* (3), 24-26.
Gale, B. T., and Klavens, R. *Formulating a Product Quality Strategy.* Cambridge, Mass.: Strategic Planning Institute, 1983.
Hartle, T. W., and Wabnick, R. "Are College Costs Rising?" *Journal of Contemporary Issues,* Spring 1983, *1* (2), 63-71.
Morgan, A. W. "Cost as a Policy Issue—Lessons from the Health Care Sector." *Journal of Higher Education,* 1983, *54* (3), 280-293.

Larry H. Litten is associate director, Consortium on Financing Higher Education, Cambridge, Massachusetts.

Rapidly escalating prices have sparked new interest in how tuitions are set and how students and their families manage to pay their bills. To facilitate intelligent discussion, we provide a framework for analyzing college costs and pricing policies.

Perspectives on Pricing

Susan Shaman
Robert M. Zemsky

We have the distinction of belonging to the only university that Edward Slosson (1910) found to have earned a profit on undergraduate education when he conducted his study of great American universities at the beginning of this century. Not Harvard, not Columbia, but only the University of Pennsylvania of the fourteen public and private institutions that Slosson surveyed reported spending less on faculty salaries than it collected in tuitions— $33 less per student, to be exact, which translates into roughly $366 per student in today's dollars. If the same ratio of tuition income to instructional salaries prevailed today, the University of Pennsylvania would have finished the 1982–83 academic year with a surplus of $3.3 million. Slosson's findings are displayed in Table 1.

Looking at Slosson's data seventy years later, we are struck by two similarities with the situation today. The first is the remarkable clustering of private tuitions around a modal price. How is it that institutions of different sizes, in different locations, and with different operating costs manage to establish nearly uniform prices? The second is the incongruity of the data themselves. That is, we do not believe that our university was either more efficient or more penurious toward its faculty than peer institutions were. Rather, we suspect that the data provided to Slosson were wrong, a suspicion that led Slosson (1910, p. x) himself to note that "university statistics are in hopeless confusion. The methods of reporting and standards of classification

Table 1. Financial Data for Fourteen American Univerities (1910)

Institution	Total Annual Income	Annual Appropriation for Salaries of Instructing Staff	Total Number of Students in University	Total Instructing Staff in University	Ratio	Average Expenditure for Instruction per Student	Minimum Tuition	Expenditure for Instruction per Student in Excess of Tuition
Columbia University	$1,675,000	$1,145,000	4,087	559	7.3	$280	$150	$130
Harvard University	1,827,789	841,970	4,012	573	7.0	209	150	59
University of Chicago	1,304,000	699,000	5,070	291	17.4	137	120	17
University of Michigan	1,078,000	536,000	4,282	285	15.0	125	30	95
Yale University	1,088,921	524,577	3,306	365	9.0	158	155	3
Cornell University	1,082,513	510,931	3,635	507	7.1	140	100	40
University of Illinois	1,200,000	491,675	3,605	444	8.7	136	24	112
University of Wisconsin	998,634	489,810	3,116	297	10.4	157	—	157
University of Pennsylvania	589,226	433,311	3,709	375	9.8	117	150	−33
University of California	844,000	408,000	2,987	350	8.5	136	—	136
Stanford University	850,000	365,000	1,583	136	11.6	230	20	210
Princeton University	442,232	308,650	1,311	163	8.0	235	150	85
University of Minnesota	515,000	263,000	3,880	303	12.8	66	20	46
John Hopkins University	311,870	211,013	651	172	3.7	324	150	174

Source: Slosson, 1910.

are so diverse that conclusions drawn from their comparisons are apt to be misleading."

Nearly twenty years after Slosson's study, our predecessor at Penn, vice-provost for administration George Brakeley, focused once more on the University of Pennsylvania to explain how colleges and universities priced their products. Brakeley had been struck by a suggestion from John D. Rockefeller, Jr., that colleges could solve their financial problems simply by charging higher prices. However, Brakeley (1931, p. 313) believed that colleges had already raised tuition faster than prudence allowed: "It's clear that tuition fees have been advanced in the past quarter of a century three or four times as rapidly as prices of commodities." He concluded that the answer lay not in further across-the-board increases in prices but rather in improving the alignment of costs and prices for specific educational programs. "Suppose," Brakeley asked (p. 315), "the University of Pennsylvania were to charge to each student the actual cost of his education rather than the flat rate of $400, which obtains in all of the schools outside the field of medicine. In the college, we should have to charge $512; in architecture, $554; in veterinary medicine, $783; in medicine, $1,031; and in most of the engineering work, well over $1,000. Even then we should not be charging the full cost, for these figures do not take into account depreciation of plant, interest on investment, and certain other factors."

Could such program-specific costs be determined? Brakeley, like Slosson, confronted the conundrum of all education cost analysis—who is to determine what is to be charged to whom? In strikingly modern terms, Brakeley sketched out (p. 317) the problem of the imaginary accounting rules: If education could be organized as a commercial enterprise, it was a matter of properly booking "the interest on the investment, taxes, a depreciation charge for buildings and contents, the operating costs, and a reasonable margin for profits and surplus." Since the resulting figure of such full-cost education would be prohibitive, Brakeley settled for charging students only on the basis of actual operating cost. However, recognizing the difficulty of "segregating the total university-costs as among instruction, research, and public service," Brakeley closed (p. 318) by calling for the development of "a method . . . for evaluating the cost of . . . research so that it may properly be charged its fair share of university expenditure, and instruction [may be] relieved of that part of the burden." No modern president wrestling with the vagaries of the rules of federal indirect cost recoveries or the implications of federal regulations— such as Office of Management and Budget Circular A-21 on indirect cost accounting—has said it better.

The pricing and cost issues that faced higher education in 1931 still dominate discussions of educational financing today: Tuition is rising faster than general prices, price sensitivity is increasing among students and their families, and the differentiation of tuition charges so that the price of a specific educational program more closely reflects its operating costs remains problematic. Unfortunately, even the fuzzy vocabularly of 1931 is still in use. Colleges and universities use the term *educational costs* to mean the cost of instruction, the total cost to the institution of the educational experience provided to the student, and the cost of tuition, room, board, and incidentals to the student and the student's family. Institutions still speak indiscriminantly about educational *expenses,* the *price* of an education, the *full cost* of an education, and the student's *budget.* The result is near hopeless confusion as to what is being talked about and why.

Our purpose in this chapter is to define what we in higher education mean by *price* and *price increases.* Necessarily, we will have to spend some time defining educational costs, and, like our colleague Brakeley, we will draw on the experience of the University of Pennsylvania over the last decade for examples of prices and pricing policies.

Prices

The best way to make sense of current discussions of educational prices is to recognize that colleges and universities price their products much as the automobile industry prices new cars. Indeed, a year in most colleges just about equals the cost of a new car—in some cases, a rather stripped-down compact; in others, a loaded full-sized sedan. Institutions of higher education share with automobile makers a sense that products can be priced in terms of a base, a package of options, and a variety of discounts. With this as our starting point, we offer four definitions of educational prices: base price, sticker price, discount price, and cash cost.

Base Price. Every institution publishes a schedule of tuition and fees for its programs and courses. The published tuition and fees constitute the institution's base price. Every full-time student understands that the base price is the stated tariff for the set of courses and classwork in which he or she is engaged. The institution understands that the base price is the tuition and fee rate that it can compare with the base price of the previous year and that it will almost certainly use to derive next year's base price.

Sticker Price. Unlike the base price, which can be compared with the price of a stripped-down car, the sticker price represents the price of the total educational package. While the sticker price includes the base price, it also includes the price of related items—room, board, fees, and incidentals. The sticker price is the item that families usually understand to be the full cost of a year's education. The sticker price is also what financial aid officers mean when they talk about the student budget. Needless to say, the sticker price varies with the options included: The student commutes or lives in a triple room, the student takes twenty-one meals a week or only ten, the student's home is 50 miles from campus or 500 miles away. Within some institutions, the sticker price can vary widely; within others, it virtually does not vary at all.

Discount Price. While the sticker price is a sobering figure at all but the least costly commuter schools, it is not necessarily the price actually paid for the educational package that the student selects. For a large proportion of students and their families—for the majority at some institutions—the actual price that they pay is represented by the discount price. It is easy to imagine that the families of two freshmen who enter the same college pay different amounts for their children's education. It would be the same, albeit less conceivable or acceptable, if two families drove identical Oldsmobiles, but they had paid considerably different amounts to the same dealer. The discount price, the net price of an education, is what families spend by the time they have finished paying for the student's college degree. The most straightforward discount price is produced by the award of grant-in-aid, a merit or athletic scholarship, or need-based scholarship aid. The result is to reduce the sticker price directly and often substantially.

A grant funded out of an institution's operating budget acts both as a price reduction and as a revenue reduction, and it is clearly analogous to a retailer's price discount. In contrast, scholarships funded through the restricted budget—endowments and gifts—represent a price discount to the student, but they have no effect on the institution's operating revenue. Finally, grants from outside the institution, principally from the federal government, are like manufacturers' rebates, because the institution, acting as the dealer, gives the student a general discount, whose value is reimbursed to the institution with an appropriate handling fee.

Like grants, educational loans often contribute to the price discount. They come in a number of forms from a variety of sources—institutional, private, and governmental. The loans themselves are generally not discounts unless they include some forgiveness of principal. However, interest reductions and in-school interest subsidies represent real price enhancements. In fact, during the late 1970s, when inflation was measured in double digits, the real value of deferred loans was considerable.

One last contribution to discount price is the provision of a campus job. In the case of federally sponsored College-Work Study (CWS), only a small proportion of the monies come from institutional funds. Yet, even when work availability is fully funded by an institution, it usually represents a significant price support to the student at minimal cost to the institution. Often, the jobs that students fill would have to be filled by others. At the same time, only a college or university would need to offer or could offer many of these jobs—jobs in areas directly related to student and academic life involving part-time work with flexible hours that fit into academic schedules.

Cash Cost. While price, especially the discount price, of college can affect a student's decision to apply, it is, as Tierney has shown (1982), increasingly the out-of-pocket cost of education that shapes decisions to enroll. Regardless of price, most families are concerned with the cash costs of college—the amount of money that the family must contribute out of its own resources during a given year. Cash costs are those educational expenses actually accounted for in the family's checkbook. Unlike the discount price, cash costs can be inflated by peripheral expenses that the sticker price does not cover. Where students share these costs in the form of postgraduation debt repayment, the cash costs include deferred costs as well.

In Table 2, we give examples of each price for two universities—one a state flagship, the other a private research university—and for two hypothetical families, (A) one that qualifies for a Pell Grant and other forms of financial aid and one (B) that does not qualify for financial aid. In both cases, it is assumed that the student arranges a guaranteed student loan (GSL) of $2,500. In our example, the cash cost of attending a high-priced private institution does not differ for the family of the high-need student from the cash cost of attending a lower-priced public institution.

Cost and Pricing Policies

How much does it cost an institution to provide its educational product? We can report no appreciable progress since Brakeley in developing useful rules of cost allocation. Despite the considerable efforts of accountants and the National Association of College and University Business Officers (NACUBO), academic managers still do not have reliable measures of the fixed or variable costs associated with specific educational activities. NACUBO, in particular, holds considerable responsibility for this lacuna, since it values accounting elegance over managerial efficiency. To be sure, all institutions now identify some expenditures as intended for instructional purposes to distinguish them from funds for sponsored research or for organized activities. In public institutions, particularly in institutions governed by state funding formulas that entitle institutions to public monies in proportion to their instructional activities, there is a clearly stated intention to segregate instructional budgets. Nevertheless, in all but the smallest colleges, public or private, the blending of purpose and hence of cost still makes a mockery of attempts at precise cost accounting. Not only is it impossible to separate instructional costs from research and service costs, but fixed costs remain indistinguishable from variable costs.

Institutions can relate changes in total institutional costs to changes in the institution's base price. Discussions of costs are often part of a larger discussion of price and the institution's need for additional revenue to balance its budget. It is in this setting that we will examine and define the pricing policies that most institutions use, singly or in combination, to maintain their financial stability.

Proportional Cost Pricing. Under proportional cost pricing, the base price tuition income is assumed to cover a fixed proportion of the real cost of an education. Increases in teaching and related operational costs require a corresponding increase in tuition prices, even where the endowment or other revenues can supply the necessary income. This strategy assumes that, even

Table 2. Educational Costs of Two Hypothetical Families at Public and Private Institutions Based on 1982–83 Prices

Family A – With Financial Need

Price		State University			Price		Private University		
		Funds' Source		Discount			Funds' Source		Discount
Base Price	$2,150				Base Price	$8,000			
Sticker Price	$5,400	Family	$1,300	$ 0	Sticker Price	$12,500	Family	$ 1,300	$ 0
		Grants	1,750	1,750			Grants	7,100	7,100
		CWS	0	0			CWS	900	900
		Loans	2,350	850			Loans	3,200	850
		Total	$5,400	$2,600			Total	$12,500	$8,850

Cash Costs $1,300
Deferred Costs $2,500 and Interest

Cash Costs $1,300
Deferred Costs $3,350 and Interest

Family B – Without Financial Need

Price		Funds' Source		Discount	Price		Funds' Source		Discount
Base Price	$2,150				Base Price	$8,000			
Sticker Price	$5,400	Family	$3,050	$ 0	Sticker Price	$12,500	Family	$10,100	$ 0
		Grants	0	0			Grants	0	0
		CWS	0	0			CWS	0	0
		Loans	2,350	850			Loans	3,200	850
		Total	$5,400	$2,600			Total	$12,500	$850

Cash Costs $3,050
Deferred Costs $2,500 and Interest

Cash Costs $10,150
Deferred Costs $ 2,500 and Interest

Family: Parents' contribution and summer savings. Grants: Pell, state, institutional. Loans: GSL and others.

though educational costs cannot be separated accurately from other institutional obligations, it is possible to identify increased instructional expense at the margin.

Externally-Indexed Pricing. Under externally-indexed pricing, increases in the price—tuition—are set to mirror changes in the external economy as measured by the Consumer Price Index, the Implicit Price Deflator, or some index of disposable income. Using this strategy, the institution seeks to hold constant the proportion of family income spent on higher education. In the past, when externally indexed pricing failed to raise sufficient revenue to balance the budget, the resulting deficit was offset by enrollment increases.

Peer Pricing. Peer pricing is a common strategy among nonprofit organizations. Under peer pricing, a college or university sets and increases its base price in a manner that keeps it comparable with base prices at peer institutions. The most prestigious institutions determine the maximum tuition rate. To remain truly competitive, an institution assumes that it must also change its price discounts so that they match those of peer institutions. A variant form of peer pricing occurs when an institution attempts to gain market advantage by setting its price below that of its principal competitors.

Value-Added Pricing. Under the value-added pricing strategy, tuition is set to reflect the expected market value of an education over the course of a student's career. Typically, when the anticipated remuneration is high, the base price is set correspondingly high, regardless of the actual cost of providing the eduction.

Residual Pricing. Residual pricing allows the institution to determine its expense budget and all other income items first. Then, it sets tuition rates so that tuition income is sufficient to balance the budget. Residual pricing disregards the distinction between instructional and other costs and allows tuition income to cover any unmet expenses.

Mandated Pricing. Common among public institutions and private institutions that operate publicly subsidized programs, mandated pricing sets a base price that reflects the explicit or institutionally perceived perferences of legislatures and public agencies. Often, these mandated prices result from public policy decisions that combine several pricing rationales (Van Alstyne, 1977).

In the quarter century following World War II, most institutions applied a simple pricing axiom: Minimize increases in the base price. Frequently, tuition increased every second or third year. This pattern reflects both the low rate of inflation and increased public expenditures for higher education. At the same time, the nation's most expensive and best-endowed institutions dramatically increased their price discounts, instituting complex as well as inherently expensive systems of need based aid. In the 1960s, the federal government further increased the availability of price discounts by becoming higher education's dominant third-party payer. We estimate that, at the beginning of this decade, the sticker price of a college education at a high-priced private college or university was paid for in the following proportions: 65 percent by family funds, 11 percent by institutional discounts, 14 percent by federal and state assistance, and more than 8 percent by GSLs.

The 1970s witnessed rapid increases in base prices and the end of uniform prices within individual institutions. The immediate cause of such price differentiation was the phaseout of capitation grants to schools training health professionals, particularly physicians, dentists, and veterinarians. In the early 1970s, the base price of these programs was often similar to the base price of undergraduate education at the same institution, but by 1981–82, medical school tuition was often 25 percent higher, and in some cases more than 250 percent higher, than tuition in the undergraduate college. As Table 3 shows, the need to keep instructional income constant despite the loss of federal capitation led to as much as doubling or tripling of medical school prices at some institutions between 1977 and 1982.

An Institutional Example of Pricing Policies

Each of the pricing policies just described has figured in the setting of tuitions at the University of Pennsylvania over the last ten years. In 1973, tuition was very similar in each of Pennsylvania's several schools. Only two of its eleven principal programs charged $200 more or less than the basic undergraduate rate. Tuition for the Wharton M.B.A. program ($3,150) exemplified value-added tuition, while the relatively low tuition ($2,300) for Pennsylvania residents in the School of Veterinary Medicine reflected a substantial state appropriation for the operation of that school.

As Table 4 shows, tuitions at the University ranged in 1981 from a low

Table 3. Medical School Tuition and Fees at Ten Institutions

Institution	1976–77	1981–82	Change 1977–1982	Ratio of Medical to Undergraduate Tuition and Fees 1981–82
University of Illinois[a]	$2,892	$ 8,108	180.4%	3.14
Washington University	3,450	6,840	98.3%	1.13
Johns Hopkins University	3,849	7,822	103.1%	1.11
University of Virginia[a]	3,919	7,046	79.6%	1.80
Columbia University	4,424	9,045	104.5%	1.34
Stanford University	4,470	8,340	86.6%	1.16
Cornell University	4,750	9,000	89.5%	1.28
University of Pennsylvania	5,000	9,490	89.8%	1.38
University of Rochester	5,385	9,246	71.7%	1.50
George Washington University	7,100	15,111	112.8%	3.60

[a] Out-of-state tuition and fees
Source: Association of American Medical Colleges

Table 4. Prices at the University of Pennsylvania:
Change in Full-Year Tuition, Fall 1973 to Fall 1981

School	1973	1973	1974	1975	1976	1977	1978	1979	1980	1981	1981
					Indexed 1973 = 100						
Wharton MBA	$3,150	100	105	106	115	124	133	165	188	216	$ 6,810
Undergraduate	2,700	100	106	115	127	139	151	178	203	234	6,315
Graduate Faculties	2,900	100	107	121	128	140	152	179	204	235	6,810
Law	2,900	100	105	112	126	137	154	182	207	238	6,905
Medicine	2,900	100	109	122	157	190	199	257	287	316	9,150
Dental Medicine	2,900	100	109	122	157	190	199	297	356	409	11,870
Veterinary	2,300	100	143	139	183	208	230	308	277	300	6,905

of $6,315 for undergraduates to a high of $11,870 for students in dental medicine. The increase in undergraduate tuition (11.2 percent per year) largely reflects a combined policy of externally-indexed and peer pricing. The increases in dental medicine (19.3 percent per year) and in medicine (15.5 percent per year) reflect a residual pricing strategy, which has been justified by the value added associated with both degrees. The increasing cost of veterinary education, despite increased state assistance, propelled veterinary tuition upward an average of 14.7 percent per year. Among the major professional schools, only the law school maintained externally-indexed pricing over the course of the decade.

Conclusion

We offer three observations in conclusion. First, trends toward the differentiation of base prices by program and by other disaggregations, such as level of study, will continue. Employing pricing strategies based on both program costs and value-added, complex institutions have already set widely divergent tuitions in their various schools.

Second, competitive price discounting will intensify throughout this decade of shrinking enrollments. Hoping to attract highly qualified students to their campuses, some institutions are offering large merit scholarships to selected applicants. Other institutions are applying unusual discounting techniques, such as substantial discounts for siblings who attend the school with an older brother or sister. Widespread use of such discounting could threaten the concept of need-based aid—a concept developed to promote access to the diverse educational offerings of this nation.

Third, for most families, discussions of college costs and pricing policies are decidedly academic. The problem that most families face is that higher education has become an extraordinary expense. At selective private colleges, for example, the average sticker price—tuition, room, board, travel, and incidentals—rose from $5,750 in 1976 to $9,070 in 1980, while the average family's per-year cash costs rose from $4,470 to $5,880 over the same period. Despite these increases, the average family's share of the bill for higher education at these institutions actually declined from 77.7 percent in 1976 to 64.8 percent in 1980. The difference was made up largely by the federal government's program of guaranteed student loans—in effect, a transfer of financial responsibility from the family to their student children and the federal government. By 1982, undergraduates at the University of Pennsylvania were borrowing the equivalent of 23 percent of their tuition bills through the GSL program.

The dilemma that faces institutional policy makers in the 1980s is how to charge prices that are high enough to guarantee educational quality. The fear is that declining federal support, high levels of student debt, and decreasing numbers of high school graduates will dramatically increase the family's price sensitivity and willingness to shop for a bargain. One possible solution is to draw yet another lesson from the makers and sellers of automobiles—direct provision of low-cost financing, which makes the purchase of a higher education possible despite the higher sticker price. The University of Pennsylvania has adopted this approach by creating the Penn Plan Agency, a kind of educational GMAC which provides families with long-term financing for tuition costs at the university. We expect future discussions to focus less on pricing and more on financing mechanisms.

References

Brakeley, G. A. "Tuition and the Student's Share of the Cost of Education." *Educational Record,* 1931, *12,* 312–321.
Slosson, E. E. *Great American Universities.* New York: Macmillan, 1910.
Tierney, M. L. "The Impact of Institutional Net Price on Student Demand for Public and Private Higher Education." *Economics of Education Review,* 1982, *2* (4), 363–383.
Van Alstyne, C. "Rationales for Setting Tuition Levels at Public Institutions." *Educational Record,* 1977, *58,* 66–82.

Susan Shaman is associate director of planning analysis at the University of Pennsylvania and has worked in planning at Temple University and Carnegie-Mellon University during the last ten years.

Robert M. Zemsky serves as both the University of Pennsylvania's chief planning officer and as the director of its Higher Education Finance Research Institute. A professor of educational finance, he currently directs the College Board's Comprehensive Undergraduate Enrollment Planning Project and the National Institute of Education's study of the Impact of Federal Policy on Training and Education in the Private Sector.

A number of issues must be considered when specifying and interpreting the empirical results of an enrollment demand model and when using these results in pricing decisions.

Using Enrollment Demand Models in Institutional Pricing Decisions

William C. Weiler

Starting with Ostheimer (1953), many researchers have analyzed the demand for higher education institutions among potential enrollees. Hyde (1978), Jackson and Weathersby (1975), and Weinschrott (1977) have reviewed the literature. Formal models of enrollment demand behavior have been constructed to study the effects of labor market conditions (Freeman, 1976), attendance costs, and federal financial aid policies on student access and choice behavior. Nearly all these studies have used national data bases, and nearly all have been applied to groups of institutions, not to single institutions or to state systems of institutions. However, a number of institutional policy issues can be illuminated with enrollment demand models estimated at the institutional level. My purpose in this chapter is to discuss the issues that must be considered in specifying and interpreting the empirical results of an enrollment demand model for a single institution and to show the uses of enrollment demand analyses in pricing decisions. Examples from the University of Minnesota will be used to illustrate the results.

Specification and Interpretation Issues

The basic economic model of student decision making is the human capital model. This model posits that students invest in education to increase their future monetary incomes and to increase the value to them—"utility" in economists' terms—of their leisure activities (Becker, 1962). The decision of the student and the student's family to invest in higher education is based on a comparison of the benefits of attendance, primarily postschooling income, and the costs, primarily the cash outlays required for attendance. The student chooses the alternative where the difference between benefits and costs is the largest. Hence, attendance demand should vary with the cost of attendance, financial aid, labor market conditions that affect the expected benefits, such socioeconomic variables as ability and family income, and psychological variables related to goals and motivation that can affect the probability that benefits will be realized, the ability to pay the costs of attendance, or both.

Economic theory based on the human capital model predicts that increasing attendance costs (tuition, fees, books, dorm charges, and so forth) will reduce attendance rates because an increase in costs reduces the difference between the benefits and the costs of attendance. Increasing financial aid increases attendance because it reduces the net price of attendance. Ability and income should both be related positively to attendance. Labor market variables have ambiguous effects on enrollment behavior (Hoenack and Weiler, 1979). Consider, for example, the effect of the current wage of non-college graduates: First, this wage influences estimates of future earnings if the student does not attend. The expected effect is negative. Second, this wage influences the value of time spent in college out of the labor force. Again, the expected effect is negative. Third, this wage also influences the income that the student could receive while working part-time and attending college. The expected effect is positive. Although it is often alleged that a higher opportunity cost of college has an unambiguously negative effect on attendance, there is no a priori basis for inferring that the third influence is dominated by the first two.

It is tempting to include in the analysis only those variables that institutional administrators can control, such as tuition and financial aid awards. However, other variables that influence students' choices and that vary within the data sample used for estimation must be included in the statistical model to ensure unbiased estimates of the effects of the variables that can be controlled. Fortunately, many of the variables that can influence attendance demand do not vary within the samples commonly used for estimation. For example, such cost components as books and living expenses ordinarily do not vary within the samples, or they cannot be measured for groups of individuals. Many psychological variables, such as confidence, practicality of outlook, or social interaction skills, also do not vary within grouped samples and can therefore be ignored.

The analyst who estimates enrollment demand models for individual institutions must also consider variables that can alter the enrollment choices among institutions as well as the choice of attendance or nonattendance. The most important of these variables measures the degree of substitution between other institutions and the analyst's institution, because the human capital theory predicts that some students who would otherwise choose the analyst's institution will attend a substitute if the cost of attending the substitute decreases. Two components of the cost of substitutes are cash outlays—tuition and fees less financial aid—and proximity—the cost of time and travel to substitutes. Measures of both cost components should be included as separate variables in the analysis when they vary within the estimation sample.

The symbolic representation of the enrollment demand equation for a single institution is

(1) $$E = f(T, TOTHER, LM, COMP, FINAID, SES)$$

where E = enrollment, T = tuition and fees at the institution, $TOTHER$ = cash outlays at substitute institutions, LM = labor market conditions, $COMP$ = proximity of substitute institutions, $FINAID$ = financial aid at the institutions, and SES = other socioeconomic variables, such as sex, income, and ability. Equation 1 can be estimated using data samples of individuals or groups gathered at one point in time (cross section) or grouped data gathered over time (time series), although the particular variables that vary with enrollment and that must be included in the sample will differ. For example, in a grouped time series sample, ability varies only with average aggregate ability of potential students over time, and it is likely to vary only slightly within the sample. Cash costs of attendance at all institutions are the same for each individual in a cross sectional sample, but proximity costs are not; hence, the latter can be included but not the former. Both cash and proximity costs vary across a time series sample, since substitute institutions can open or close over time, but in a time series sample, tuitions are often highly correlated at all institutions, so that it may not be possible to obtain separate estimates of the effects of each. It is possible to include only the institution's own tuition in the model and to interpret the estimate of its coefficient as the effect of a concomitant tuition change at all institutions. (We can expect this effect to be negative, since a concomitant reduction in the cost of attendance at all institutions increases attendance at one's own institution by more than the losses to substitute institutions.)

The dependent variable also varies with the type of data sample. With grouped data, the dependent variable is specified as the ratio of enrollment to the number of high school graduates who meet the institution's admission requirements. For a sample of individuals, the dependent variable takes either of two values representing the choice of attendance or nonattendance at the school. For all types of samples, the unknown parameters can be estimated by multiple regression analysis, although researchers who analyze individual data may wish to use a technique more appropriate to binary dependent variables, such as logit or probit analysis (Pindyck and Rubinfeld, 1981).

The type of sample needed depends on how the results are to be used. For decisions related to future enrollments or budgets, time series analysis is preferred, because the variables in equation 1 related to business cycles, such as labor market conditions, also vary over the forecast period. Cross sectional data samples can be used to estimate the impact of pricing policies, financial aid policies, or both on individual students.

The same theory and methodology can be applied to the transfer behavior of students enrolled elsewhere and to the behavior of students at one's institution who are deciding whether to continue. It is important to include social and psychological factors in models of continuation behavior estimated with individual data, since research on this topic has shown the importance of these variables (Bean, 1982).

With grouped data, the dependent variable for transfer behavior is the proportion of students transferring in year t. The numerator can be either the total number of transfers to the institution or the number from a subset of other institutions, such as all local junior colleges. The denominator should be the potential transfer student population (such as total enrollments, all sophomores, or all sophomores and juniors) in the previous year at the institutions from which transfer students could come. The analyst can estimate a single equation for all transfers or separate equations for transfers from different groups of institutions. For continuation behavior, the dependent variable can be year-to-year progression ratios for cohorts of students—for example, the proportion of freshmen in year t still enrolled in year $t+1$—or an aggregate continuation rate—the proportion of students in year t still enrolled in year $t+1$. The former measure requires estimated equations for each cohort, while the latter requires estimation of only one equation. The choice depends on the data that are available and on the likelihood that the effects of the independent variables differ across the cohorts.

Enrollment Forecasting

One obvious use of demand equations estimated from a time series sample is in forecasting an institution's enrollments (Hoenack and Weiler, 1979). The enrollment rate can be forecast if we know the values of each independent variable. Enrollment is computed by multiplying the estimated rate by the expected value of its denominator. However, we do not know the future values of the variables on the right-hand side or the value of the denominator. These values can be estimated using trend techniques, multiple regression equations with these as dependent variables, or alternative policy options that administrators may explore, such as changes in the level of tuition or changes in relative tuition for lower- and upper-division students. The choice between trend techniques and additional regressions depends on whether a theory relating other variables to the unknown variable is available. For example, many theoretical analyses have related labor market variables to general economic conditions. These analyses can be used to specify equations for the prediction of labor market variables if we remember that the variables on the right-hand side in the auxiliary regressions must also be forecast to generate an enrollment forecast. Trend techniques can be used when no theory is available, as in estimating historical grade-to-grade progression ratios for elementary and secondary school students.

Formal models of enrollment demand provide three advantages over other forecasting methods that do not explicitly consider the separate effects of each variable that can influence enrollment. (Wing, [1974] surveys enrollment forecasting methods commonly used in individual institutions.) First, alternative forecasts based on alternative values of the right-hand side variables are easy to obtain. Hence, the typical what-if questions of administrators are easy to answer, and the assumptions underlying the forecast are stated explicitly.

Second, unbiased estimates of the effect of each variable on enrollment and the standard errors of these estimates are obtained. The unbiased estimates produce a forecast centered in the distribution of the estimated forecast error. In addition, the analyst can determine which variables significantly affect enrollment, and he or she can also calculate the contribution of the variance of each parameter estimate and the standard deviation of the residuals to the estimated forecast error. The size of the forecast error determines the degree of flexibility that administrators should maintain in decisions that depend on the enrollment level. The minimum forecast error is the standard error or the residuals, so that such a decomposition shows the proportion of the forecast error that cannot be reduced. This allows administrators to evaluate the uncertainty of the estimates relative to the uncertainty inherent in student behavior that is not captured by the model. The second error component is particularly useful in preserving flexibility in decision making.

Third, the magnitudes of the estimated parameters enable administrators to determine the relative effects on enrollments of the variables that they can control and of the variables that they cannot control. Specifically, administrators can observe the potential control that they have over enrollments through the use of pricing policy to influence enrollment decisions or to counteract demographic or economic trends.

Tuition Policy

The rationale for setting an institution's tuition depends on whether it is public or private. Private institutions, nearly all of which have more applicants than admitted students, generally set tuition levels according to their goals for the number and quality of students, subject to the levels of tuition set by other institutions that compete for the same types of students and to the expected tuition revenue net of their financial aid awards. (The next section of this chapter discusses the application of enrollment demand analysis to this problem.) In public institutions, tuition levels are set in three basic ways. The first is an ad hoc adjustment process "that might best be described as incremental pricing" (Viehland and others, 1982, p. 335). The second is to base adjustment on an index, such as the Higher Education Price Index. The third is to base tuition on institutional costs, a concept that is gaining adherents (Johnson, 1979; Viehland and others, 1982; McCoy, 1983).

Only a few schools have considered tuition policies incorporating rates that vary by instructional costs for undergraduate students in different programs and levels. Later in this chapter, I will discuss the use of enrollment demand analysis to estimate the results of a policy of basing tuition on instructional costs for student level and program, and I will illustrate the results with data from the 1983-84 pricing policy at Minnesota. A cost-related pricing policy could have substantial benefits for subsidizers of higher education. (Hoenack and Weiler [1975] discuss the benefits of cost-related tuition policy and the issues that must be addressed in implementing the policy.) Institutions would receive a more accurate picture of student demand for program offerings, because it would be based on the benefits of programs after taking account of their different costs. The decisions of subsidizers regarding selective deviations from a constant proportion of tuition to instructional costs would also be better informed than they are under a system in which the relation between tuition and instructional costs in each program is arbitrary.

The most important analysis for the cost-related policy lies in estimating the effects of changes in tuition on enrollment. In particular, the behavioral responses to tuition changes are different for eligible high school graduates who are deciding whether to enroll, for enrolled undergraduate students who are deciding whether to continue, for students enrolled elsewhere who are deciding whether to transfer, and for graduates who are deciding whether to enroll in a graduate or professional program. In addition, changes in tuitions by program may encourage some students who are already enrolled to transfer to other programs within the same institution.

Most institutions can obtain good estimates of the effects of tuition on attendance for all new freshmen as a group. However, tuitions in different programs have not been differentiated in the past, or at least they have been very highly correlated. Hence, it is unlikely that tuition variables for each program can be entered in separate estimating equations for new freshmen in each program. Thus, analysts may be able to estimate only one equation with an aggregate of new freshmen as the dependent variable. However, since the tuition differences for new freshmen under a cost-related tuition policy are not likely to be substantial, any of the tuition rates can be used to estimate the aggregate numbers of new freshmen. In fact, institutions which have tuitions that differ by program usually maintain a single rate for freshmen or lower-division students regardless of program.

Most institutions can also derive good estimates of the effect of tuition on continuation behavior, however it is measured. These institutions will find that the effect of a given percentage change in tuition on attendance will be much smaller for continuing students than it will for new freshmen, because continuing students have already invested time and effort in the institution and because their educational objectives are more focused than those of new freshmen. In terms of the human capital model, the additional benefits of continuation are likely to outweigh the additional costs of the tuition change for most students already enrolled.

Since potential transfer students generally have a number of institutions from which to choose, the effect of a change in tuition on potential transfers should be similar to the effect on new freshmen. The statistical significance of the parameter estimates will depend on the degree of measurement error in the dependent variable created by the uncertainty in defining the potential transfer student population. (Measurement error in the dependent variable of a multiple regression does not produce biased estimates of the parameters, but it does increase the standard error of estimate and hence the standard deviations of the estimated coefficients.)

If continuing students can transfer to other programs within the institution, then the institution's analysts will also want to estimate changes in the internal distribution of students that changes in tuition will produce. However, few institutions have had sufficient variation in tuition in different programs over time to provide a data sample from which analysts can estimate these effects. In any case, they are likely to be small, because changes in tuition across undergraduate programs are likely to be small.

For some categories of students, enrollment demand analysis can be very effective in estimating the effect of tuition charges, while the response of other categories may not be estimable at all. This is a common problem in the use of enrollment demand analysis. While it would be ideal to estimate all effects precisely, the results do show policy makers the areas that they need to monitor closely if a new tuition policy is implemented (Hoenack and Weiler, 1975). The effects of cost-related pricing on the quality of professional and graduate students in an area of particular importance in enrollment. These programs have the highest instructional costs, and a given percentage increase results in relatively large dollar increments in tuition levels.

Optimizing Policy Makers' Objectives

Enrollment demand equations are also used in models for optimizing subsidizers' objectives regarding enrollments of students of different academic ability or different socioeconomic categories. Enrollment demand models estimated from cross sectional data can be used to show the results of allocating a given total institutional subsidy (or total amount of financial aid) in various ways to the various categories of students. Elliot (1980) describes a model for the allocation of financial aid to individual students that maximizes the institution's net tuition revenue given an enrollment demand function that shows how attendance varies with financial aid. Ehrenberg and Sherman (1982) maximized an objective function based on the quality of the institution's student body subject to a subsidy constraint and to functions defining student quality and admissions and financial aid decisions. Hoenack (1971) specified a similar model in which the policy maker uses institutional pricing policy to optimize goals related to the mix of students from different socioeconomic backgrounds. Hoenack's model is probably more relevant to public institutions, while those of Elliot and of Ehrenberg and Sherman are more relevant to private institutions. The example that follows is closest to Hoenack's model, but it would be easy to adapt it to the other models by adding additional constraints.

Suppose that we have n socioeconomic or quality categories of students. If TS = total institutional subsidy, C = institutional cost per student (assumed to be the same for all students), E_i = enrollment from category i, T_i = tuition charged to students in category i, F_i = institutional financial aid per student in category i, and X_i = a vector of other variables influencing enrollment of students in category i, the total subsidy is the difference between total costs and revenues:

(2)
$$TS = \sum_{i=1}^{n} (C + F_i - T_i) E_i$$

Enrollments in each of the n classes are forecast from

(3)
$$E_i = f_i(T_i, F_i, X_i)$$

where the f_i's are estimated enrollment demand functions. The institutional administrator's problem is to set $T_1, \ldots, T_n$ and $F_1, \ldots, F_n$ to maximize objectives regarding enrollments subject to the constraint on the size of TS and to the constraint that enrollments are determined by equation 3. This is an optimization problem of the form

maximize $g(E_1, \ldots, E_n)$
subject to the $n + 1$ constraints

$$TS - \sum_{i=1}^{n} (C + F_i - T_i) E_i \geq 0$$

$$E_i - f_1(T_1, F_1, X_1) = 0$$
$$\vdots$$
$$E_n - f_n(T_n, F_n, X_n) = 0$$

where $g(E_1, \ldots, E_n)$ is the symbolic representation of the administrator's enrollment objective. For example, if the administrator wishes to maximize total enrollment, the optimand is

$$g(\cdot) = \sum_{i=1}^{n} E_i$$

If the objective is to attract equal enrollments in each group, the objective is to maximize the smallest E_i subject to the constraint that all E_i's are equal. This can be done by maximizing the previous objective function with the additional constraint

$$E_1 = E_2 = \cdots = E_n$$

Use of this model for the allocation of financial aid to individuals can require the analyst to confront the issue that a value of financial aid for a student at a given institution is observed only for students who apply for admission and financial aid, who are accepted, and who enroll. The amount of aid awarded to a student is a function of socioeconomic characteristics that determine the student's financial need. However, the student's decision to enroll is related to the financial aid that the student receives. Hence, the amount of financial aid and the enrollment decision are determined simultaneously by separate relationships representing student and institutional behavior. To determine whether an estimate of the effect of financial aid in the enrollment demand equation can be computed, the analyst must specify both relationships to determine whether the coefficients in the demand equation are identified. Manski and Wise (1983) exemplify this approach. Identification of the unknown coefficients in a system of simultaneously determined relationships is a property that logically precedes estimation of the coefficients. Identification of the coefficients of one equation in the system is determined by the answer to the question, Could the observed data sample have been generated by only one set of values of the unknown coefficients, by just a few sets of values, or by an infinite set of values? The coefficients of the equation are called *just* (or *exactly*) *identified, overidentified,* or *not identified,* respectively. In the last case, the coefficients cannot be estimated with any data sample. For a discussion of identification and of estimation methods for simultaneous equations models, see Pindyck and Rubinfeld (1981).

Institutional Budgets and Staffing

In this section, I will discuss how pricing policy and the resulting enrollments estimated by enrollment demand analysis can be used in institutional planning and long-range budget estimation.

Budgets. The essence of financial planning in institutions of higher education lies in identifying sources of revenue and expenditures and in estimating how both vary with variables under the institution's control—the variables defined by Hopkins and Massy (1981) as primary planning variables—and with socioeconomic conditions outside the institution's control. Sources of general instructional revenue for higher education institutions are tuition and fees, state subsidies, federal subsidies (primarily student aid), indirect cost recoveries, and investment income. It is obvious that the tuition and fee income for both public and private institutions depends on enrollments, but the level of enrollments in public institutions tends to depend much more on student demand than on institutional admissions decisions. Hence, enrollment demand analysis of the type discussed here is likely to be most useful for budget planning in public institutions. Hopkins and Massy (1981) discuss other models for estimating enrollments that may be useful for private schools. Enrollment plays a key role in determining the values of many other planning variables.

Institutional enrollment forecasts serve two financial purposes. First, the number of students determines total tuition revenue. Second, many institutions receive funds from subsidizers based directly or indirectly on enrollment. State funds for public institutions tend to be based on enrollment. In some states, private institutions also receive enrollment-related public funds. All institutions also receive public funds indirectly from federal or state financial aid awarded to students.

While I argued earlier that a cost-related tuition policy could provide benefits to subsidizers of higher education, it is unlikely that individual institutions would embrace such a policy unless it benefitted them directly. Most institutions will probably find that a cost-related tuition policy increases both enrollments and tuition revenue more than a policy that does not differentiate tuitions by program (Hoenack and Weiler, 1975, 1979). Where tuition is not cost-related, lower-division students pay a higher fraction of their average instructional costs for tuition than upper-division students do, but all undergraduate students pay a higher fraction than graduate and professional students. Assuming that the institution retains the same overall ratio of tuition revenue to total instructional costs, a cost-related tuition policy results in lower tuition for lower-division students, slight increases or decreases for upper-division students, and substantial increases for graduate and professional students.

The expected impact of the resulting changes on enrollment and tuition revenues can be described by reference to the elasticity of enrollment demand with respect to tuition or to the percentage change in enrollment for a given percentage change in tuition. The studies cited in this chapter and our work at Minnesota indicate that the elasticity for lower-division students ranges from 0.5 to 1, which means that lower-division enrollments will increase at least one half of the percentage by which their tuition rate falls; the total tuition revenue collected from these students may not change at all, but any percentage decline is almost certainly limited to half of the percentage change in the tuition rate. The elasticity of upper-division students is lower—about 0.25. This low elasticity, accompanied by small tuition changes, implies that both enrollment and tuition revenues will change only slightly for these students. Graduate and professional enrollments have an elasticity of zero, because applications exceed admissions in these programs. Enrollments in these programs will not change, and tuition revenues will increase substantially as a result of large increases in tuition. Hence, both total institutional enrollments and tuition revenues will almost certainly increase under a cost-related tuition policy.

Table 1 depicts the impact on enrollment and tuition revenue of a cost-related tuition policy at the University of Minnesota. The estimates of enrollment in Table 1 are based on models similar to those of Hoenack and Weiler (1979). The table compares the effect of retaining the tuition policy in effect at Minnesota in 1982–83 (Policy 1) with the effect of gradual implementation of a full cost-related policy (Policy 2) over a period of four academic years while maintaining the average increase in tuition rates constant. Gradual implementation of a cost-related tuition policy has three advantages. First, students already enrolled are not hit with large increases in tuition. Second, the impact on institutional revenues is gradual, and planning can proceed in an orderly fashion. Third, uncertainties associated with the estimation process make gradual implementation less risky. The results show that the impact on enrollment and tuition revenues is favorable for Minnesota. Minnesota began implementation of Policy 2 in the 1983–84 academic year. The results for other institutions will depend on their estimated demand elasticities and on changes in their tuition rates during implementation of a cost-related tuition policy.

The change in tuition revenue resulting from implementation of a cost-related tuition policy is only a small part of the impact of such a policy on the institution's total revenue. The most substantial part of the change results from the effect of changes in enrollment on legislative appropriations. If an institution receives its overall average cost per student on a formula basis from the state legislature, all additional enrollments are funded at this overall per-student amount. However, the additional enrollments produced by cost-related tuition are all in the lower division, where average instructional costs per student are almost certainly less than the institution's overall average. In addition, the marginal cost of additional lower-division students is likely to be less than the average costs. Hence, the institution can receive an increase in its appropriation that is substantially larger than its actual additional cost. Note

Table 1. Estimated Enrollment and Tuition Revenue from Alternative Tuition Policies

	Total Enrollment		Total Tuition Revenue	
	Policy 1: Tuition Undifferentiated by Costs	Policy 2: Fully Cost-Related Tuition	Policy 1: Tuition Undifferentiated by Costs	Policy 2: Fully Cost-Related Tuition
1983–84	55,849	55,319	$71,597,000	$71,672,000
1984–85	51,536	55,259	72,688,000	74,519,000
1985–86	47,921	53,556	67,909,000	72,264,000
1986–87	45,269	53,003	64,543,000	71,751,000

that even an institution funded on a formula differentiated by student level can benefit from a cost-related tuition policy, since it still gains the difference between its marginal cost and the average cost that it receives from the legislature.

The legislative appropriation also reflects the demand of legislators for provision of higher education opportunities to constituents. Thus, even if the institution is funded on a formula basis, the legislature can change the formula or not fully fund it whenever the formula allocation deviates substantially from its demand. Like consumer demand, legislative demand is a function of the price that the legislature must pay and of the income (tax revenue) that it has to spend. Legislative demand is also influenced by constituent pressure for the various outputs that the legislature can provide. Symbolically, we can represent legislative demand as

$$(4) \qquad A = g(C - T,\ TAXREV,\ EP,\ OP)$$

where A is the legislative appropriation to the institution; $C - T$ is the difference between the average cost per student and the tuition collected per student or the net price per student that the legislature must pay; $TAXREV$ is total state tax revenue; EP is enrollment as a proportion of the total voting population, which represents the strongest interest group of constituents demanding that the legislature provide higher education services; and OP is a proportion where the numerator is the size of an interest group for other services, such as the elderly. For a derivation of legislative demand based on interest group influences, see Hoenack (1983a); Hoenack (1983b) provides an application to higher education. Since the strength of interest group influence on legislative demand can be independent of costs, the legislature has less incentive to differentiate a funding formula on the basis of instruction costs. This outcome enhances the potential benefits of a cost-related tuition policy.

Equation 4 shows that the institution's legislative appropriation depends in a complex way on tuition policy and on the effect of tuition policy on enrollments. Tuition affects the appropriation directly through the net price variable and indirectly through the effect of tuition on the EP variable. However, the situation is complicated by the fact that institutional costs per student (the variable C in the net price variable) also vary with E and hence indirectly with tuition policy. The three relationships relating enrollments, institutional costs, and the appropriation must be estimated simultaneously (Hoenack, 1983b).

Table 2 shows estimated legislative funding for the University of Minnesota under the tuition policies that produce the results shown in Table 1. Comparison of Tables 1 and 2 shows that the institution's tuition revenue is $7.2 million higher in 1986–87 than it would have been if a cost-related tuition policy had not been implemented and that the legislative appropriation is nearly twice that amount, $14.2 million. Again, the results for other institutions will depend on their estimates of the appropriation, enrollment, and cost relationships discussed in this chapter.

Staffing. Enrollment demand analysis can also aid in analysis of the size and composition of an institution's faculty (Hoenack and Weiler, 1977). Most institutions can use faculty flow models that allow estimation of the effects of various faculty personnel policies on hiring, promotion, and retirement on the composition of the institution's faculty by age, rank, sex, race, tenure status, and other characteristics. To use these models, the analyst must know the total size of the faculty each year in the simulation period and institutional parameters reflecting personnel policies.

Enrollment demand analysis enters the picture through the effect of enrollment on the size of faculty. While the relationship between number of students and faculty may not be fixed, the available evidence suggests that the student-faculty ratio in American higher education, adjusted for inflation, institutional mix, and other institutional expenditures, has remained nearly constant since the 1930s (O'Neill, 1971) and that short-term deviations from the long-term value have resulted from the inability of institutions to adjust the number of faculty instantaneously to the number of students (Freeman, 1971). I suspect that most institutions can estimate a simple trend relationship between enrollment and faculty to forecast their total faculty size over the simulation period. Hence, the institution can use a faculty flow model to simulate both the direct effect of personnel policies and the indirect effects of tuition policies and other policies designed to influence enrollments on faculty characteristics. Such analysis will inform administrators of the potential control that they have over the size and composition of their faculty without use of measures that can create fear and uncertainty in the faculty. For example, Hoenack and Weiler (1977) found that a cost-related tuition policy would produce a larger faculty size, more new hires, and a lower fraction of tenured faculty for the University of Minnesota than policies that reduced the probability of achieving tenure or that encouraged early retirement.

Enrollment Effects of Institutional Closure

Enrollment demand analysis can also be applied to individual institutions by decision makers in regional higher education coordinating agencies.

Table 2. Estimated Legislative Appropriations from Alternative Tuition Policies

	Policy 1: *Tuition* *Undifferentiated* *by Costs*	*Policy 2:* *Fully* *Cost-Related* *Tuition*
1983–84	$207,500,000	$209,700,000
1984–85	199,900,000	205,900,000
1985–86	190,600,000	200,600,000
1986–87	182,400,000	196,600,000

Given current demographic trends, one important use of such analysis is in estimating the enrollment redistribution that would result from closure of one or more institutions (Weiler and Wilson, in press).

If we assume that the demand function in equation 1 is linear in each of the variables that influence enrollments, we can write a set of demand functions for attendance at each of $m-1$ institutions in the region plus the mth choice of nonattendance as follows:

(5) $$E_i = a_{io} + \sum_{j=1}^{m-1} a_{ij}T_j + \sum_{k=m}^{n} a_{ik}X_{k-m+1} \qquad i = 1, \ldots, m$$

where the T's are tuition rates at each school, the X's are the other variables influencing enrollment demand, and the a's are parameters estimated using multiple regression. To use equation 5 in predicting the enrollment effects of closing institution k, we let T_k'' be the tuition at which $E_k = 0$. From the kth equation in equation 5, T_k'' is defined by

(6) $$E_k = a_{kk}(T_k - T_k'')$$

For any other option q, this change in the cost of attendance at k results in an enrollment E_q' defined by

$$E_q - E_q' = a_{qk}(T_k - T_k'')$$

If we substitute from equation 6 for $T_k - T_k''$ and rearrange terms, we get

$$E_q' = E_q - a_{qk}\frac{E_k}{a_{kk}} = E_q - \frac{a_{qk}}{a_{kk}}E_k$$

Hence, if institution k is closed, the proportion of enrollees at k who select any other option q is the ratio of the estimate of the effect of tuition at k on attendance at q to the effect of tuition at k on attendance at k.

This method, based on behavioral analysis of enrollment choices, is likely to produce better estimates of the enrollment redistribution effects of institutional closure than models that redistribute students to the remaining institutions in proportion to total enrollments in the remaining institutions, with or without the assumption that nonattendance is an option. For these choices actually to be made, the second choices of those enrolled at the closed school must be identical to the first choices of those enrolled at the other schools. This is unlikely, because the characteristics of students attending the closed school, including their proximity to the other schools, are not likely to be identical to the characteristics of students who chose the other options before the institution was closed. The method based on enrollment demand analysis explicitly considers relative substitutability, because the parameter estimates are based on students' actual choices.

Summary

This chapter began by examining the specification and interpretation issues involved in the application of enrollment demand analysis to individual institutions. Next, it discussed the use of enrollment demand analysis in estimating the impact on enrollment of changes in the structure and level of tuition, and it described the role of enrollment demand models in an institution's long-range financial and personnel planning. It observed how tuition and financial aid policy can be used to optimize the objectives of institutional decision makers regarding the size and socioeconomic composition of enrollment, and it concluded by showing how enrollment demand analysis can be used to estimate the enrollment redistribution effects of institutional closure.

References

Bean, J. P. "Student Attrition, Intentions, and Confidence: Interactive Effects in a Path Model." *Research in Higher Education,* 1982, *17* (4), 291-320.

Becker, G. S. "Investment in Human Capital: A Theoretical Analysis." *Journal of Political Economy,* 1962, *70* (5), 9-45.

Ehrenberg, R. G., and Sherman, D. G. "Optimal Financial Aid Policies for a Selective University." Department of Economics, Cornell University, 1982.

Elliot, W. F. "Financial Aid Decisions and Implications of Market Management." In J. B. Henry (Ed.), *The Impact of Student Financial Aid on Institutions.* New Directions in Institutional Research, no. 25. San Francisco: Jossey-Bass, 1980.

Freeman, R. B. *The Market for College-Trained Manpower.* Cambridge, Mass.: Harvard University Press, 1971.

Freeman, R. B. *The Overeducated American.* New York: Academic Press, 1976.

Hoenack, S. A. "The Efficient Allocation of Subsidies to College Students." *American Economic Review,* 1971, *61* (3), 302-311.

Hoenack, S. A. *Economic Behavior Within Organizations.* New York: Cambridge University Press, 1983a.

Hoenack, S. A. "A Structural Model of Legislative Choice in Financing Higher Education." Minneapolis: Management Information Division, University of Minnesota, 1983b.

Hoenack, S. A., and Weiler, W. C. "Cost-Related Tuition Policies and University Enrollments." *Journal of Human Resources,* 1975, *10* (3), 332-360.

Hoenack, S. A., and Weiler, W. C. "A Comparison of the Effects of Personnel and Enrollment Policies on the Size and Composition of a University's Faculty." *Journal of Higher Education,* 1977, *48* (4), 432-452.

Hoenack, S. A., and Weiler, W. C. "The Demand for Higher Education and Institutional Enrollment Forecasting." *Economic Inquiry,* 1979, *17* (1), 89-113.

Hopkins, D. S. P., and Massy, W. F. *Planning Models for Colleges and Universities.* Stanford, Calif.: Stanford University Press, 1981.

Hyde, W. D., Jr. *The Effect of Tuition and Financial Aid on Access and Choice in Postsecondary Education.* Denver: Education Commission of the States, 1978.

Jackson, G. A., and Weathersby, G. B. "Individual Demand for Higher Education: A Review and Analysis of Recent Empirical Studies." *Journal of Higher Education,* 1975, *46* (6), 623-652.

Johnson, J. C. "An Analysis of the Relationship Between Instructional Costs and Differential Tuition Levels." *Journal of Higher Education,* 1979, *50* (3), 280-288.

Manski, C. F., and Wise, D. A. *College Choice in America.* Cambridge, Mass.: Harvard University Press, 1983.

McCoy, M. "Differential Tuition at the University of Colorado." Paper presented at the Regents' Budget Workshop, University of Colorado, Office of Planning and Policy Development, August 1983.

O'Neill, J. *Resource Use in Higher Education.* Berkeley, Calif.: Carnegie Commission on Higher Education, 1971.

Ostheimer, R. H. *Student Charges and Financing Higher Education.* New York: Columbia University Press, 1953.

Pindyck, R. S., and Rubinfeld, D. L. *Econometric Models and Economic Forecasts.* (2nd ed.) New York: McGraw-Hill, 1981.

Viehland, D. W., Kaufman, N. S., and Krauth, B. M. "Indexing Tuition to Cost of Education: The Impact on Students and Institutions." *Research in Higher Education,* 1982, *17* (4), 333–343.

Weiler, W. C., and Wilson, F. S. "Prediction of the Enrollment Effects of Institutional Closure." *Research in Higher Education,* in press.

Weinschrott, D. *Demand for Higher Education in the United States: A Critical Review of the Empirical Literature.* Santa Monica, Calif.: Rand Corporation, 1977.

Wing, P. *Higher Education Enrollment Forecasting: A Manual for State-Level Agencies.* Boulder, Colo.: National Center for Higher Education Management Systems, 1974.

William C. Weiler is associate director of the Management Information Division, Office of Management, Planning, and Information Services at the University of Minnesota.

Price setting for tuition and fees is a critical element in college and university budget building. A number of factors influence pricing decisions and suggest different strategies for income generation and resource allocation.

Priorities, Planning, and Prices

Timothy Warner

Pricing decisions—and the processes that lead up to them—play a powerful role in the setting of institutional goals and priorities. From the perspective of the university budget officer, a number of pricing decisions must be made in the course of developing a budget, and setting the price for undergraduate education is just one of them. Prices to be paid for faculty salaries, library acquisitions, and maintenance are other decisions that an institution must face. These decisions are important because the educational outcomes that flow from them help to determine the character and success of the institution. While the focus of this chapter will be on the issues behind the pricing of tuition, it is important to understand how tuition fits into the context of the other pricing decisions that a university must face.

One way to understand these pricing decisions and how they are made is to think of the academic institution as a production process subject to a series of cost and revenue markets (Hopkins and Massy, 1981). Under such a model, the cost markets include those for faculty, staff, equipment, library books, and buildings. In each of these markets, the institution must pay a price—for example, the salaries of teaching and support personnel, the cost of laboratory equipment, and the price of the energy needed to run the buildings. On the revenue side, the university must set prices for each of its three principal products—instruction, research, and philanthropy.

On the cost side of the budgetary equation, different price rationales determine how much should be paid for each item of expense. For faculty, the guiding rationale can be to maintain salaries at a level equal to or slightly above that of competitors. For staff, institutional policy may call for salaries to be set at the midpoint of the outside labor market. Other prices are the result not of an institutional rationale but are determined for the institution simply by what appears on an invoice from an external supplier. For example, utility costs are what the electric company charges, and the only way in which they can be altered significantly is by political lobbying or by conservation measures.

On the revenue side, each of the institution's three products—instruction, research, and donations—carries its own price. For instruction, tuition is the relevant price. For research, a series of prices is charged, including prices for both the direct and indirect costs of conducting research. For donations, the price is the amount required to give particular recognition to a donor's contribution. Because much more will be said later in this chapter about tuition, a brief description of the prices associated with the other two outputs is in order.

With respect to research, the sponsoring agencies and organizations will pay the direct costs—salaries, equipment, and travel—for doing the work. Most sponsoring groups will also pay the indirect costs of research, but on a cost-recovery basis. In some situations, the indirect costs are too large for the sponsor to bear. At this point, the payment mechanism for indirect costs changes from the recovery of actual costs to a price charged by the institution for some portion of overhead—an amount that it feels will allow it to remain competitive for research funding. Underrecovery of indirect costs implies a policy decision to share costs with the sponsoring entity. Such a decision, if taken for the long term, has significant implications for the role of research in the institution. By sharing costs, the institution diverts funds that, under a full cost-recovery basis, would have gone to other parts of the institution. Over time, such a tilt in resources could affect the character of an institution by drawing funds away from nonresearch areas to areas where research support was significant. Although the outcomes of policy in this area will vary by institution, the point is that cost recovery has important policy implications, whether indirect costs are recovered through the traditional method of cost reimbursement or through the price mechanism.

Donations are not always regarded as having prices, and it may be difficult to think of donors as a potential market. However, donors do pay for the satisfaction of seeing their dollars go to a cause they can support. Some of these satisfactions carry a specific price—named chairs and buildings, public listing as a contributor of a specified amount, and so forth.

Forces That Affect Prices

For each of the revenue markets, the budget planner must consider the impact of three forces on the development of prices: the institution's market position, its public image, and its ambition. Like the charges of an atom, each of these forces can have a positive, negative, or neutral impact on price. Each force can push prices higher or lower or have no effect at all. Unlike the charges of an atom, which are always fixed—that is, a proton always carries a positive charge—these forces can also reverse direction, depending on the condition of the institution, the market, or both. For a high-quality institution that enjoys substantial demand for its services, a strong market position can put an upward pressure on price; so, too, can public perception of the institution if the institution is perceived to be strong but underpriced for the benefits that it provides. Institutional ambition can also push up prices. The desire to get better, to add new programs, to increase services to students and faculty, or to speed up progress toward an academic goal usually puts upward pressure on prices. However, if these ambitions are pursued within the context of internal budget reallocation or increased productivity, they do not necessarily lead to price increases.

These three forces can also exert downward pressures on prices. For example, if an institution's market position has deteriorated over time, then the rate of price increase is likely to slow. Similarly, if the institution's public image has been hurt or if its plans and ambitions change, potential price increases may be curtailed. Although costs have not gone down in recent years, they can go down in some categories of expenditure, and this can reduce the growth rate of institutional prices. However, whether such cost decreases actually result in lower prices depends on the institution's internal budgeting strategy and its competitive pricing position.

In considering pricing policies for tuition, the model described by Shaman and Zemsky in Chapter One is an appropriate starting point. This model shows that pricing policies rely on one or some combination of six basic tuition strategies: Under proportional cost pricing, tuition is set to cover a fixed portion of the institutional operating budget. Under externally-indexed pricing, tuition increases are tied to changes in general economic indicators, such as the GNP deflator or personal disposable income. Under peer pricing, tuition rates are set in relation to the range of tuition levels at competing institutions. Under value-added pricing, tuition is set to reflect the market value of a degree from the institution over time. If the income that can be expected is high, the price is correspondingly high, even if the actual cost of education is modest. Under residual pricing, tuition is set so that total tuition income is sufficient to balance the budget. Thus, the decision about tuition is the last to be made when a budget is built. Finally, under mandated pricing, tuition reflects the mandated preference of legislative policy.

Each of these pricing strategies is fairly straightforward. For the institution that uses a single strategy, some internal analysis is necessary to translate the principles into a pricing plan. For example, a college that uses only the residual method has to develop its whole budget before it can determine tuition. The institution that pegs the price of tuition to an external economic indicator needs to analyze how that indicator has changed over time. Where a single strategy is used, the appropriate measure is simply inserted into the process or the equation.

In institutions that rely on more than one strategy to set prices—and this is probably the vast majority—the decision-making process assumes a different character. Instead of approaching price setting in a formulaic manner, these institutions must give judgment a much greater role. Whether they realize it or not, most university budget planners make reference to most of these six strategies in setting a price and then apply some judgment to their analysis. They may not think each strategy through in a systematic way, but they do pay some attention to all six, at least intuitively, as the process unfolds. Three of the six strategies stand out as generally the most important in the development of pricing decisions: proportional cost pricing, externally indexed pricing, and peer pricing. Understanding each of these pricing methods, the interrelationships between them, and the important issues behind them will help the reader to understand how pricing decisions are made.

Proportional Cost Pricing

Any discussion of using the costs of undergraduate education as a basis for pricing must first consider costs universitywide, then determine how those costs relate to undergraduate education. In an institution where faculty do no research, where there are no graduate students, and where there are no supplementary programs, the definition of educational cost is relatively simple. In such cases, undergraduate educational costs can be defined as the institution's total operating budget. Thus, the average cost of education per student is the institutional operating budget divided by the number of students.

Joint Costs. In universities where faculty do research and where there are graduate students, the problem of determining proportional costs is complicated by the phenomenon of joint costs. Joint costs are costs that can be allocated to more than one cost objective at any given time. They are costs that produce two or more goods or services at the same time or that produce a benefit on which another benefit is highly dependent. For example, where should a faculty member's salary be allocated when he is working on a research problem with a graduate student and he will use the results of that research in an undergraduate lecture course? Should that portion of his salary go to undergraduate instruction, to graduate education, or to research? The answer is certainly yes. What the dilemma of this particular situation reveals is that the decision on allocation of costs has to be somewhat arbitrary and that a set of commonly accepted rules is needed. For the costing purposes of government-sponsored research, the rules in the Office of Management and Budget's Circular A-21 apply. For other research, institutional personnel will have to make these judgments.

Differential Pricing. Another problem posed by the proportional costing of undergraduate education lies in determining the cost of different academic programs or majors. It is clear that some educational programs cost more than others (Bowen, 1980). For example, it costs more to turn out a physics major than it does to turn out an English major, both in the direct costs and in the overhead support costs. Whether the institution is an undergraduate college or a university, this fact has implications for pricing policies. The most direct implication is the potential for differential pricing, a concept that involves making tuition charges reflect the cost of instruction in any given major program. This concept is already followed to some degree in the pricing of graduate programs. The most dramatic example, perhaps, is the difference at many institutions between the tuition charged to medical students and the tuition charged to humanities students.

The prospect of moving to a fully differentiated pricing structure at the undergraduate level presents an all-encompassing budgetary problem with significant implications for the academic, administrative, and financial functions of a university (Yanikoski and Wilson, in press; McCoy, 1983). From an academic perspective, differential pricing removes the subsidy that students in lower-cost programs pass on to students in higher-cost programs. The result is greater price equity. This is certainly a desirable outcome, but it is not without cost. One administrative cost that it increases is the cost of financial aid administration. Operating in a differential pricing environment means changes in the way in which aid is delivered, and in the short run this means that aid office expenses will increase.

Differential pricing has some other significant implications for management. For example, what does it imply for centralized and decentralized budgeting? Does it mean that academic departments will become more involved in developing their own tuition rates? If departments have a say in developing prices, will they be able to change their cost structure or negotiate their own overhead? Some departments may choose to become more cost-efficient. This will foster internal competition. Other departments, particularly those well positioned in the market, may raise prices to cover inefficiencies that the consumer can never expect to understand. Differential pricing will also involve considerable discussion and formulation of program costs, overhead allocation, and rules by which these costs are translated into the prices that are charged. The process of developing these understandings is likely to be a costly effort in and of itself.

From a financial perspective, differential pricing does not always increase revenue. While prices may be made to reflect cost differences more accurately, the resulting changes will not necessarily increase overall revenue unless a greater fraction of costs is captured through programs where prices increase. Further research on price differentiation, with particular emphasis on its internal implications, would be of considerable interest to budget planners.

Unbundling. Another cost issue that can result in significant changes from traditional pricing policies is the unbundling of costs. Unbundling is essentially the separate pricing of academic services that were sold in the past as a complete package. Unbundling can be of two types, external and internal. External unbundling involves sharing or transferring basic academic functions, including instruction and credentialing, from universities to other social institutions, such as the media, the military, or computer software firms. Internal unbundling is generally defined as the separate purchase of instruction, advisement, evaluation, and other services from a single institution (Wang, 1975, 1981a, 1981b).

For our purposes, only internal unbundling is relevant. For particular kinds of institutions, unbundling can provide attractive ways to reduce costs and increase revenue. However, in adopting an unbundled pricing strategy, an institution must take a hard look at its goals and traditions, and it must assess the sort of campus environment that is likely to be produced by the separate pricing of services. In an academic environment that is characterized by close ties between faculty and students and that prides itself on providing a variety of services to all students, significant unbundling may change the institution's broad educational effectiveness. In contrast, unbundling may make sense for commuter institutions and for colleges with part-time non-degree-seeking students, because it would enable students to purchase just the services that they want, and their overall education bills would drop as a result.

The unbundling of pricing presents a significant budgetary challenge. Institutions with a centralized budgetary structure will have to adopt a more decentralized method of budgeting. For example, if advising services are made available for a fee only to those who want them, advising becomes a kind of auxiliary enterprise, perhaps a service center. Particularly adept managers are required if these services are to operate effectively on a break-even basis.

The unbundling of services and course offerings also has some clear academic implications. Those students who are the most independent and able will probably benefit more (or be hurt less) than the students who require advice and counseling. For unbundling to work well, some hard decisions will have to be made about what should be required for a credential and about what academic support services should be made part of the program. This decision-making process bears some resemblance to the development of safety regulations. If seat belts are the minimum legal requirement, their cost will be covered by the price of the car. But, the buyer will pay more for the automatic version and more if the car has an airbag. The same is true in an unbundled academic environment. A faculty adviser may come with the price of admission, but health services and career planning cost extra. Academic officers will need to give thorough consideration to such fundamental decisions before unbundling can be implemented.

Price Discounting. It is difficult to think about costs and prices without also considering the effects of price discounting on institutional budget development and pricing policy. Price discounting, which has become standard practice, is simply defined as the award of financial aid. This aid comes in a variety of forms. Whether students need the money or not, and whether the institution targets discounts to particular individuals or follows some other policy, the financial result of price discounting is usually the same—a lower price, and the college takes in less revenue. The only exception to this result occurs in markets with high price elasticity, where marginal costs are less than the marginal price after discounting and where demand increases as a result of discounting. As educational institutions struggle to maintain enrollment or as they attempt to sustain a particular kind of student body, the pressure to discount price intensifies. The recent inability of government financial aid programs to keep pace with institutional costs makes the situation even more difficult for budget planners. As enrollment and cost pressures continue to mount, three types of price discounting responses seem likely to be sustained, particularly among private institutions. First, for institutions with enrollment problems, price discounting for both low-income and nonneed students will continue at the expense of educational quality. Some institutions will inevitably go out of business.

Second, in institutions that do not have enrollment problems but that cannot afford to meet the financial need of every student through aid, relative price discounting will take the form of merit scholarships and financial aid gapping—that is, not fully meeting need as calculated by financial aid need formulas. This strategy allows the institution to use its limited financial aid resources more effectively by targeting some portion of those resources to high-ability students through merit scholarships. The remaining financial aid money is then spread among the rest of the students through the gapping mechanism. Institutions that use this mechanism probably do not risk going out of business. However, they must be concerned about their ability to maintain past levels of quality. One probable result of this discounting policy is an increase in the affluence of students at the institution.

Third, a small group of colleges will continue to meet the demonstrated financial need of every student. These institutions must consider the effect of this policy on their cost structure and on the subsidy that full tuition payers will have to sustain to support those on financial aid. Tuition will have to increase to cover the rising cost of the required institutional financial aid. In considering the impact of price discounting for these institutions, budget planners will find it useful to track changes in three indicators over time: total unrestricted aid as a fraction of total tuition, incremental aid as a fraction of incremental tuition, and marginal cost of aid.

Total unrestricted aid as a fraction of total tuition is defined as the portion of total tuition dollars that goes into unrestricted financial aid. As this ratio increases, both the subsidy that full payers give to less than full payers and the number of tuition dollars displaced from academic programs to financial aid increase. Incremental aid as a fraction of incremental tuition is defined as the portion of incremental tuition money that went into financial aid during the preceding year. By looking at the rate of change in this indicator over time, the budget planner can get a sense of how much of the increasing burden of financial aid is being paid by the full payers. Finally, marginal cost of aid is defined as the marginal cost to the unrestricted financial aid budget of raising tuition by one extra dollar after all other outside aid sources have been exhausted.

Externally-Indexed Pricing

While it is certain that an institution's internal economy is driven by costs, those costs—and the prices that flow from them—are dictated to a significant degree by the movements of the external economy. For the past decade, inflation has been by far the most prominent force in driving up costs in the economy at large. However, analysis of the real growth rates of a sample of high-cost private institutions shows little or no increase in enrollment while real expenses were moving up at a 2 to 3 percent annual rate. This real increase reflects an economic condition peculiar to colleges and universities. Over time, real wages in the external economy rise with productivity, which has had a long-term growth rate of about 2 percent per year. If academic salaries do not rise at the same rate, some faculty and staff can be lost to other organizations in the short run. In the long run, an academic career may lose its appeal for many.

Does this fact mean that universities can expect their costs to rise at a 2 to 3 percent annual real rate, or at the external rate of growth in productivity? There are two perspectives on this question. Theoretically, the answer is yes, as long as demand remains steady. However, some people argue that colleges and universities should take a more active role in achieving productivity savings, so that wages paid out could continue to grow at a 2 percent annual real rate, while overall costs would increase at a somewhat slower pace.

Can colleges and universities achieve productivity savings without a drop in the quality of program? The use of computers has been helpful in generating productivity increases, particularly in administrative areas. But, administrators must continue to ask the tough questions about how productivity can be increased and costs can decrease as the number of computer applications increases. On the faculty side, use of instructional technology has increased productivity. If technological changes are introduced in the proper context, productivity can improve without reducing quality. However, it has often proved difficult in both administrative and academic areas to realize savings from the installation of a new computer system because of the tremendous potential for new or improved services that the new computer makes possible.

The achievement of productivity increases or of savings has also been slowed by the increasing marginal cost of developing or discovering one new unit of knowledge. The cost of staying on the ever-advancing frontier of knowledge has become progressively more expensive over the past few decades, and there are few signs that this trend will change. As a result, the productivity savings generated through technology are eaten up by the rising cost of increasingly sophisticated research. As Massy (1982) observes, it is ironic that universities make important contributions to increased productivity in the external economy that they cannot capture themselves and that increase their labor costs by driving up salaries in general.

What do these arguments about productivity say about pricing? The immediate answer is that real increases in wages tend to push up costs, and, in the absence of productivity enhancements, they act to raise prices. If wages, hence costs, are increasing at an average real annual rate of 2 percent, then there is justification for pushing prices, hence tuition, up at about 2 percent as well. This rationale makes sense for families that can afford college out of current income. It also makes sense for families that can supplement current income with sufficient savings or that have access to financial aid. But, for families without access to an adequate stock of capital and for families that, after borrowing heavily, are just on the margin of affordability, prices will eventually outdistance their ability to pay.

Consequently, significant real increases in tuition coupled with reductions in financial aid could well lead to further pressure on enrollments. Under such a scenario, the private institutions will suffer the most. One area in this equation that bears further study is the role of savings as a major contributor to payment of college costs. Will a drop in the savings rate and a concurrent drop in available financial aid reduce ability to pay? If so, what kinds of impacts will this development have on the future pricing policies and enrollments of colleges that are just on the edge of viability?

Peer Pricing

The third set of parameters on which institutions rely in setting tuition is their position in relation to competitors. Most institutions know all too well who their competitors are, and track these institutions' pricing movements quite closely. An institution has to take care that it does not get too far behind its principal competition on price. There are three exceptions to this general rule: First, if other sources of revenue can fill in for the price variation so that the program being supported is comparable in quality to those of competitors, falling behind a bit on price will not have a measurable impact. For example, the institution that is heavily endowed can afford to keep its prices lower while maintaining a quality comparable to that of competitors, except to the degree that the public uses price as an indicator of quality and that it is ignorant of endowments and their contributions. Second, if the institution is seeking enrollment increases from a specific market segment that can be attracted by lowering price, it may be more desirable to achieve that goal than it is to keep pace with the competition. In some cases, a college may charge less to students who are part of a new program or school, since the quality of that program has not been demonstrated. Third, if there are major differences in the price discounting policies of competing institutions, the net price differential may be negligible, although the published prices vary considerably. This situation raises a number of interesting questions about the role of financial aid in making pricing decisions. It is clear that prices have increased to some extent to pay for the increasing cost of financial aid. What does this imply for future price increases? When will the level of subsidy reach a point where full payers balk? What kinds of implications does this point have for future enrollments?

Conclusions

Establishing the price to be charged for undergraduate education is just one of a number of pricing decisions that an institution must face in developing its budget. From the viewpoint of budget planners, tuition is an extremely important price, because it is usually the largest income item in the budget and because it is one over which the institution can exert substantial control. Although a number of different factors affect price, the cost structure of an institution's programs is probably the most significant. Costs can be allocated to major programs, and prices can be differentiated among those programs as a way of increasing revenue. In addition, budget developers have the option of unbundling various cost elements in order to price different educational services and programs separately.

The movements of the external economy and the actions of competitors have a tugging and pulling effect on costs and on the prices that reflect them. Institutions cannot afford to fall behind competitors for the resources that they require, such as faculty, and in the prices that they are willing to pay for these resources. However, they must make special efforts to ensure that price increases do not move up over time at rates exceeding the average family's ability to pay. Furthermore, they cannot drop behind their principal competitors for students on price unless income is available from other sources to sustain academic programs. The interplay of these counterbalancing forces makes tuition setting one of the more interesting and dynamic institutional processes.

References

Bowen, H. R. *The Costs of Higher Education: How Much Do Colleges and Universities Spend Per Student and How Much Should They Spend?* San Francisco: Jossey-Bass, 1980.

Hopkins, D. S. P., and Massy, W. F. *Planning Models for Colleges and Universities.* Stanford, Calif.: Stanford University Press, 1981.

Massy, W. F. "Financial and Business Planning at Stanford." In *Stanford University Annual Financial Report.* Stanford, Calif.: Stanford University, 1982.

McCoy, M. "Differential Tuition at the University of Colorado." Paper presented at the Regent's Budget Workshop, University of Colorado, Office of Planning and Policy Development, August 1983.

Wang, W. K. S. "The Unbundling of Higher Education." *Duke Law Journal,* 1975, *45* (1), 53-90.

Wang, W. K. S. "The Dismantling of Higher Education." *Improving College and University Teaching,* 1981a, *29* (2), 55-60.
Wang, W. K. S. "The Beginnings of Dismantling." *Improving College and University Teaching,* 1981b, *29* (3), 115-121.
Yanikoski, R. A., and Wilson, R. F. "Differential Pricing of Undergraduate Education at Comprehensive Colleges and Universities." *Journal of Higher Education,* in press.

Timothy Warner is associate provost, management and budget, at Stanford University, California.

This chapter describes how pricing decisions are made in public and private higher education, who participates, and what factors are considered.

The Politics and Practicalities of Pricing in Academe

Joseph E. Gilmour, Jr.
J. Lloyd Suttle

This chapter describes how pricing decisions are made in public and private higher education, who participates in the process, and what factors are considered in making such decisions. It is based on case studies of the tuition- and fee-setting processes at Yale University for 1982–83 and 1983–84 and in the State of Washington for the 1981–83 biennium. These cases are presented not as general models of pricing decisions in the public or private sectors but as empirical vehicles for illustrating the politics and practicalities of price setting in higher education.

Fundamental Political Process Concepts

Use of the term *politics* to describe decision making in organizations and governmental systems often connotes trickery, deception, collusion, or the blatant use or abuse of power. Yet, theorists (for example, March and Simon, 1958) have shown that models based on assumptions of rational economic man generally do not fit reality. Models which assume that behavior is political—that individuals and groups act in their own self-interest through use of various forms of informal power—are more useful for understanding and predicting behavior in complex organizations (Tonn, 1980) and govern-

L. H. Litten (Ed.). *Issues in Pricing Undergraduate Education.*
New Directions for Institutional Research, no. 42. San Francisco: Jossey-Bass, June 1984.

mental systems. Political models are particularly useful for analyzing decisions about who gets what, because disagreements tend to arise, and they must be resolved through the use of power. Thus, it is clear that political behavior is both a critical and inevitable component of decision-making processes.

Power. The essence of political behavior is power—the capacity of one person or group to control the actions of others. Social scientists have defined, categorized, and theorized about power in different ways. One of the most comprehensive treatments of power and politics was provided by Bacharach and Lawler (1980). Drawing on the work of several other theorists, these authors identified four bases of power: the control of punishments (coercive power), the control of rewards (remunerative power), the control of symbols (normative power), and the control of information (knowledge power). Control of these resources by an individual or group is derived from one or more of four different sources: office or structural position; personal characteristics, such as charisma, intelligence, verbal skills, ability to argue persuasively, or physical attributes; expertise—the specialized information that people bring to a situation; and opportunity, which derives from the informal aspects of position and which provides the incumbent with critical information or a strategic position from which to apply coercion.

Two fundamental forms of power evolve from these different sources. The first is authority, the power that derives from a person's or group's superior position; this form of power is sometimes termed *formal.* The system's structure is the sole source of authority, which may provide control over any or all four bases of power just identified. The second form of power is influence, which derives from the personalities of the actors involved, their expertise, or the opportunities afforded by their positions in relation to the flow of information or work within the system. This form of power, which is frequently referred to as *informal,* is the currency of political behavior. Unlike authority, influence is multidirectional; it can flow upward, downward, or even horizontally among peers. It is the dynamic, tactical element that is a primary source of change in social systems. It is also expandable, in the sense that the influence of a person or group can increase without an offsetting decrease in the influence of others.

Interest Groups, Coalitions, and Bargaining. While in some situations power can accrue to individuals, in most cases it is acquired, maintained, and used by interest groups and coalitions. Interest groups are groups of individuals who share a common goal or a common fate beyond their simple interdependence in the conduct of work. Bacharach and Lawler (1980) assert that organizations and political systems are networks of interest groups, each of which attempts through political actions to influence decisions that affect its position or resources in the organization. In some cases, interest groups pursue their political goals on their own; in other situations, they form coalitions with other interest groups to pursue a common goal.

Interest groups and coalitions dominate social systems because they crystallize the various interests of individual members, uniting those with the most common interests against those with the most divergent interests. The resulting conflicts are manifest in the bargaining between coalitions. The essence of bargaining is tactical action—attempts to manipulate information in order to create certain impressions, to test or evaluate the impressions given by the opposing coalition, and to assess the opponent's resolve or commitment to a given position. Tactics vary with the relative power of the opposing groups, the nature of the issue at conflict, and the level of dependence or interdependence between the parties.

While the preceding paragraphs only summarize some of the basic notions of political analysis, the concepts that they present provide a better framework for understanding price setting in higher education than economic and market factors alone.

Price Setting in the Private Sector

Income tuition and room and board charges referred to collectively as the *term bill,* constitutes more than 25 percent of total income in Yale University's annual operating budget and 40 percent of its unrestricted income (that is, exclusive of indirect costs recoveries for sponsored research). These percentages have risen gradually in recent years, since income from gifts, endowment earnings, and federal support has not kept pace with the overall growth of expenses, and Yale has had to rely increasingly on student charges as a way of achieving a balanced budget. At the same time, Yale College is one of the highest-priced schools in the country, with an annual term bill rate of almost $13,000 in 1983-84. There is growing concern that an increasing number of families may begin to feel that a Yale education is either not affordable or not worthwhile for their children. Given the critical role of tuition in the financial well-being of the university, its obvious importance to students and their families, and the attention that it receives from the media and the general public, it is clear that we need to understand the way in which political pressures operate within practical boundaries to influence tuition- and fee-setting decisions at Yale.

The Process at Yale. The price-setting process at Yale is inextricably bound up with budget planning. The politics of the pricing decision must therefore be viewed in the context of the three-step process through which the university develops its annual operating budget.

Step One: Calculating the Budget Base. To support both its short-term and long-term financial planning, Yale uses a computerized planning model that estimates each of the major income and expense items in the operating budget as well as the bottom line surplus or deficit under a given set of conditions. This model was developed in 1978 using the Educom Financial Planning Model (EFPM); in 1983, the university converted to a series of microcomputer-based models based on Lotus 1-2-3. In the first phase of the budget development process, the myriad of assumptions, estimates, and calculations that underlie the model are reviewed and updated, and an initial or base case projection of the budget for the following year is prepared. Most of this work takes place in the late summer and early fall, and it is performed by the provost and budget director and their staffs. At this early stage, the Office of Institutional Research serves as a critical source of information (for example, for comparative tuition and salary data), technical expertise (for example, in expanding and refining the model), and analytical support (for example, in examining the impact of various budgetary trade-offs and assumptions).

In recent years, the base case projection has consistently shown a deficit. This projected deficit changes constantly during the later stages of the budget development process, as new information, further analysis, changes in the financial environment (for example, changes in the expected inflation rate or the level of federal support), or changes in the university's own financial plans (for example, a decision to increase tuition more or salary less than originally assumed) compel the underlying assumptions to be refined and revised. Nevertheless, the initial projection provides an essential base for all the difficult budgetary discussions that follow, and it indicates in general terms the amount of financial pressure that the university will face over the next two or three years.

Step Two: Identifying Corrective Actions. Since the university is mandated by the Yale Corporation (its board of trustees) to achieve a balanced budget, the second and more difficult step in the budget development process is to identify ways of eliminating the projected deficit. The pricing decision generally plays a key role when modifications to the base case projection are considered, for term bill income is one of the few discretionary items in the university budget that can have a substantial impact on the bottom line. The assumption underlying the base case projection—and the university's de facto long-term pricing policy—is that the term bill rate will grow at roughly the same rate as personal income, a figure that historically has averaged 1 to 2 percent above the general rate of inflation. In recent years, the term bill price has been adjusted upward from this initial level as one means of reducing the projected deficit.

Responsibility for deciding how best to achieve a balanced budget rests formally with the University Budget Committee, an advisory committee chaired by the provost that consists of senior faculty and administrators, including the president, who meet regularly to review all budget proposals and major financial decisions. The proposals are prepared and presented by the heads of major budgetary units within the university. After the budget committee reviews and revises them, it passes them on to the Corporation for final, official approval. The Corporation rarely turns down these proposals, and yet it does far more than rubber-stamp them. It gives careful consideration to all major issues, such as pricing, and it often makes its views known to the president and the provost in preliminary discussions of the proposals that its members will be asked to approve, perhaps in revised form, at subsequent meetings.

The dean and the associate dean of Yale College prepare the annual proposal on undergraduate tuition and room and board rates and present it to the budget committee in January. The essential elements of this proposal are worked out ahead of time in private discussions between the dean, the president, and the provost, who must weigh trade-offs between the term bill price and other budgetary priorities and reach a mutually agreeable pricing decision. Throughout the process, these parties seek to be informed and influenced by a wide range of private persuasion, public pressure, and economic analyses. For example, staff from the budget office and the provost's office are consulted to ensure that all recommendations are consistent with the university's overall budget plan, while staff from the admissions and financial aid offices provide input (generally in the form of anecdotal evidence and knowledgeable opinions, not concrete data) about the actual or perceived affordability of a Yale College education. Finally, the Office of Institutional Research supplies comparative data about trends in tuition, room and board rates, and self-help levels (a combination of educational loans and term-time earnings that every student must provide before qualifying for scholarship aid from the university) at Yale and at other institutions.

The one major interest group that plays almost no role in the price-setting process is the undergraduate student body. Except for occasional articles that appear in the student newspaper during the week or so prior to annoucement of the term bill and a front-page article on the day after, student voices are seldom heard on the issue of pricing. Furthermore, students play no formal role in the university's budget-planning process, and there has been little organized political activity by students seeking to influence major budgetary decisions. In fact, there is no effective mechanism (for example, a strong student government) through which students could lobby for a particular position on pricing or any other campus issue. Perhaps the major reason for the lack of a strong student advocacy role in the price-setting process is that the student body is so diverse that it could never speak with one voice. This diversity is particularly relevant to the issue of pricing. Pricing involves trade-offs among different student interest groups — for example, financial aid students are insulated from term bill increases, but they are directly affected by increases in the self-help level, while students who do not receive aid are directly affected by the term bill level, but they are not touched by aid policies. Hence, students do not play a role in the price-setting process, and they have not expressed much interest in acquiring such a role.

Step Three: Implementing the Decision. The final and most challenging step in developing the annual budget is to implement the decisions and changes implicit in the approved budget plan. At this stage, the process through which the decisions have been made is more important than their content, for, as the literature on decision making clearly demonstrates, individuals and groups are much more likely to feel committed to a decision in which they have had a voice than they are to a decision given by executive fiat (Strauss, 1963; Vroom, 1977). Successful implementation of a decision often depends more on whether it is understood and accepted than on whether it is the right or the best decision. Yale has moved to a more open, consultative decision-making process in recent years as one means of broadening support for difficult budgetary decisions by sharing responsibility for those decisions. Nowhere is this movement more in evidence than in the case of pricing decisions, for a former dean of Yale College remarked in the mid 1970s that he never found out what the tuition level would be until he read it in the student newspaper.

On one level, implementation of the pricing decision consists simply of the announcement of tuition and room and board rates for the following year. Usually, this announcement takes the form of a press release issued soon after the Corporations's formal vote on the matter. Since the cost of a Yale College education has reached such lofty levels in recent years, the announcement is generally greeted with dismay from students, parents, alumni, and the news media. Yet, it is essential for the pricing decision to be viewed as fair, reasonable, and justifiable and for a Yale College education to be viewed both as affordable and as worthwhile. Public criticism should be kept to a minimum. For this reason, the announcement is always accompanied by an explanation of the financial pressures that necessitated the increase. For Yale, such announcements generally point out the effects of inflation, the need to provide real increases in faculty salaries, the rising cost of need-based financial aid, and the need to refurbish the university's physical facilities, which have suffered from deferred maintenance policies over the past decade. The tuition announcements normally are accompanied by announcements on other major budgetary issues, such as financial aid policies and salary increases for faculty and staff.

Price Setting at Yale in 1982-83 and 1983-84: A Case Study. A close examination of the process by which the term bill level was set for the 1982–83 and 1983–84 academic years will help the reader to understand the three-step process just outlined and its political underpinnings. It will also reveal how and why the process varies from one year to the next.

1982–83. In 1981–82, like virtually every other private institution in the country, Yale began to feel the impact of Reagan administration cutbacks in support for student financial aid and to anticipate even more drastic cuts in following years. To plan a response to these funding reductions, the provost appointed a small group of senior-level administrators to examine past trends and future options in the areas of tuition, enrollment, and student aid. This task force was chaired by the dean of undergraduate admissions, and its members included an associate dean of Yale College, an associate dean of the Graduate School, the university director of financial aid, and the director of institutional research. The task force delivered its findings and recommendations to the officers and the Corporation at the end of the fall term. Its report served as background for discussions and decisions about pricing and financial aid policies in 1982–83 and beyond (Yale University, 1982).

The task force compiled evidence to show that, at least at the undergraduate level, Yale did not appear to be about to price itself out of the market for the most capable students, although there was some indication that Yale and other prestigious, high-priced schools were competing for a shrinking pool of applicants. It also concluded that the greatest threats to Yale's policy of need-based financial aid were posed by two external developments, which were largely beyond the university's control—continued steep cuts in federal support for student aid and changes in financial aid policies at other institutions (for example, if other Ivy League schools abandoned their policies of need-based aid, the proportion of aid students in Yale's applicant pool would probably increase). Various assumptions about the likelihood and probable impact of these developments were examined, and the conclusion was that a significant increase in university-funded student aid was needed. For example, a projected 10.5 percent increase in the term bill rate coupled with the most likely assumptions about decreases in federal funding and increases in the number of students qualifying for need-based student aid left a projected deficit of approximately $1 million in the Yale College budget. There were three alternatives for eliminating this deficit: larger increases in the term bill level, changes in financial aid policies, or substantial allocations of other university resources to the undergraduate college.

The reallocation of $1 milion to the Yale College budget was not politically feasible given the overall financial strain at the university. The dean of Yale College therefore presented a proposal to the budget committee for maintaining existing financial aid policies by raising the term bill price by 13.5 percent and the self-help level by 12.1 percent. The recommended increases were well above the 10.5 percent increases assumed in the base case projection, and they were high by recent historical standards. The primary justification for the dean's recommendations was the strong and nearly universal commitment to meet the full demonstrated need of all admitted students so as to ensure that Yale would remain accessible to all qualified students without regard to their abilities to pay. The dean also noted that a term bill increase on the order of 13.5 percent was reasonable given the high quality of a Yale College education, and he anticipated that even these prices probably would have little effect on the size or quality of the applicant pool, since Yale's term bill and self-help levels would be in line with those at other Ivy League institutions.

The budget committee reviewed the dean's proposal carefully and revised it before passing it on to the Corporation. The committee raised the recommended tuition increase to 14 percent, and it lowered the proposed increase in the average self-help level to 10 percent. The bottom line remained unchanged. There were two reasons for these changes. On the one hand, updated information indicated that Yale's proposed term bill increase was slightly below the average increase at other Ivy League schools, while the proposed self-help increase was somewhat higher than average. Second, the budget committee, anticipating the concerns of the Corporation, raised questions about the ability of the families of current and future students to pay the rising cost of a Yale College education. However, further analysis revealed that median family incomes had risen at almost exactly the same rate as the Yale term bill in recent years (Suttle, 1983). The Corporation approved this revised proposal at its meeting late in January 1982.

1983-84. By the time the process for deciding the 1983-84 term bill rate got under way late in 1982, both Yale's financial condition and the general health of the nation's economy had improved significantly. To be sure, the projected university budget still showed a deficit, but it was smaller than it had been in previous years. Cutbacks in federal support were still foreseen, but the worst fears of one year earlier had not been realized. While Yale's tuition and self-help levels were high, they did not appear to be causing serious shifts in the applicant pool. Finally, although the tuition increase still would be above the anticipated inflation rate, it would be well below the levels of recent years. Furthermore, no significant changes in university policies or priorities were planned. As a result, the pricing decision received much less attention from the budget committee, the Corporation, and even the media than it had a year earlier, and a proposal by the dean of Yale College to raise the term bill rate by 10.1 percent and the self-help level by 9.5 percent was accepted with relatively little discussion and no modifications.

The process for setting 1983-84 prices was less comprehensive and intense than it had been in prior years for several reasons. For one thing, the price-setting process is cyclical. Information accumulates through the learning and memory of the major participants. Absent significant turnover among senior administration, the process can assume a certain understanding of the data and a familiarity with the political pressures. The analytic work thus becomes easier both to do and to explain, since it consists primarily of updating tables containing historical trend data or comparative prices. For another thing, there was less financial pressure in 1982, both outside and inside the university.

Price Setting in the Public Sector

Over the years, tuition and fees charges in the State of Washington have been low, ranking considerably behind charges in the seven states— California, Illinois, Indiana, Michigan, Minnesota, Oregon, and Wisconsin— with which Washington has traditionally compared itself. Tuition and fees had not increased in the three fiscal years prior to the 1981-83 biennium, the period that we examine in this public sector case. These years had seen a significant increase in the Consumer Price Index, and there was general agreement among all parties to the tuition- and fee-setting process that fees would have to increase. The question was by how much and on what terms. No one foresaw that, before the tuition and fee price-setting process was completed, Washington's economy would go into a serious tailspin or that fees would increase from 35 to 79 percent above base levels.

The Process in the State of Washington. The tuition- and fee-setting process in Washington, which is dominated by the governor and the legislature, is remarkably open. It includes four basic steps, which begin the November before each biennium.

Step One: Council for Postsecondary Education (CPE) Recommendations. The Council for Postsecondary Education, the state's higher education coordinating agency, is charged with calculating the instructional operating cost for each tier of higher education — research universities, regional universities, and community colleges — prior to the beginning of each biennium. These cost calculations form the basis for the council's tuition and operating fee recommendations to the governor and the legislature. The staff effort in making these calculations and in formulating tuition and fee recommendations to the Council is substantial. Yet, this effort involves only a cursory examination of the availability of student financial aid, and it considers the impact of the state economy and other financial considerations only in the most global terms.

The Council holds a public hearing on the fees at which testimony is taken; this testimony is made part of the public record. While many interest groups testify (for example, students, faculty, institutional administrators), most believe that the hearings are a prelude to the decision-making process, which take place in the executive and legislative branches. Thus, their motivation is either to introduce new concepts or to contain damage.

Step Two: Governor's Recommendations. Throughout the fall, the Office of Financial Management (OFM) formulates the governor's budget, which is submitted to the legislature on December 21. The tuition- and fee-setting process for higher education is integral to budget construction by the OFM, since the state constitution requires the governor to submit a balanced budget to the legislature. Without clear knowledge of revenues, such as from tuition and fees, the governor cannot meet this constitutional requirement. While the governor's budget includes a statement on tuition and fee assumptions, changes in tuition and fees must be made through a separate piece of legislation.

It is in this stage that the most extensive financial and political analysis is done. Because of the balanced budget requirement, the OFM considers a variety of factors in determining the governor's recommendations for tuition and fee increases. These factors include the projected revenue from all sectors, based on current rates; the budgetary needs of all state agencies, assuming current funding levels; employee salary and cost-of-living increase requirements; areas in which budget increases must be provided; and areas in which budget reductions and revenue increases can be considered. The process admits of trade-offs, and the trade-offs are not isolated to higher education. Although the governor's recommendations were changed substantially by the legislature in the 1981–83 biennium, in most biennia the recommendations stand. Despite the importance of the governor's recommendations, there are no public hearings, and few persons know what the recommendations are until they are transmitted to the legislature as part of the budget package.

Step Three: Legislative Review and Passage of Tuition and Fees Bill. After the legislature reviews the governor's budget and the companion tuition and fees bill, hearings are held. The hearings are open, and testimony is heard from a wide range of interest groups (for example, CPE, legislative, gubernatorial, and other staff; institutional administrators; students; faculty; and private citizens). This testimony is taken seriously. Throughout the legislative process, the trade-offs that the governor has already considered are debated, and legislative staff closely track the tuition and fee bill's course and its impact on the budget. Staff also carry out additional analyses in the course of the legislative session, although this analysis tends to be less extensive than that conducted by the OFM. Finally, a bill is passed that sets tuition and fees and associated policy for the following biennium.

Step Four: Setting of Fees. Individual boards for the public four-year institutions and the State Board for Community College Education approve tuition and fee levels as part of their institution or system budget approval process in late spring. Aside from noncredit course and special fees, this approval is a pro forma passage of the fees that the legislature has established.

The 1981–83 Biennium: A Case Study. Table 1 lists the principal tuition and fee issues considered by the major players in the fee-setting process prior to a bleak revenue forecast in December 1980. The major issues concerned the terms of the increase, not the amount. All participants agreed that fees had to increase and that the increases proposed by the CPE were reasonable in view of inflation and fee levels in states with similar types of institutions. The issues under discussion included an automatic tuition and fee escalator, so that in future biennia fees could float automatically with changes in the instructional operating cost in the various institutional sectors; an institutional board option to increase fees by as much as 10 percent over base fees; and a phase-in of the proposed increases of 75 percent in the first year and 25 percent in the second.

The primary opposition to these proposals came from students, who argued strongly against the automatic fee escalator and preferred to trust their fortunes to the legislature each biennium. Ironically, supporters of the concept had seen themselves as allies of the students, because an automatic escalator would make the increases more gradual. Students rejected the 75 percent–25 percent tuition and fee increase scheme proposed by the CPE and advocated a 50 pecent–50 percent increase instead. Students also opposed the board option to increase base fees by 10 percent. In this, they were seconded by everyone but the University of Washington, with which the proposal had originated. Opponents believed that implementation of the concept would result in steadily spiralling increases for all institutions. Finally, community college students strongly urged that their tuition and fees be raised by only $34 per year

Table 1. Initial Positions on 1981–83 Tuition and Affected Fee Recommendations Adopted by Affected Groups in the State of Washington

	Council for Postsecondary Education (CPE)	Public Four-Year Institutions[a]	Community Colleges	Four-Year Students	Community College Students	Governor	Legislature
Tuition and Fee levels	CPE levels	CPE levels	CPE levels	CPE levels	11 percent increase, not 33 percent recommended by CPE	CPE levels	Higher than CPE levels
Automatic Tuition and Fee Escalator	Yes	Yes	No comment	No	No	Yes	Yes
10 Percent Operating Fee for Local Governing Board	Yes	No, except University of Washington	No	No	No	No	No
75-25 Phase In	Yes	Yes	No comment	No—50-50	No—50-50	Yes	Yes

[a] Includes University of Washington, Washington State University, Central Washington University, Eastern Washington University, Western Washington University, and Evergreen State College.

Source: Council for Postsecondary Education, 1981.

(11 percent) instead of by the $102 (33 percent) recommended by the CPE. In the end, they were turned back by conservative members of the council, who believed that the time had come for community college students to pay reasonable user fees.

When the state's December revenue forecast was made public, it became clear that the amount of the tuition and fee increases recommended by the CPE and endorsed by the governor would not be adequate. The forecast projected a state deficit exceeding $1 billion for a $9 billion budget. Table 2 compares the total academic year tuition and fee rates for 1978-81 with the CPE recommendations and the legislatively determined increases for 1981-83. While the legislative increases were made on a relatively small tuition and fee base rate, they were still substantially greater than the inflation rate, and they served to move Washington's higher education fees much closer to the average for the seven comparison states.

The process by which the legislature considered the tuition and fee increase issues was highly emotional and political. It began when an aggressive member of the governor's staff proposed even larger increases than the legislature ultimately adopted. This proposal led to a hard and bitter fight in the legislature that pitted a united higher education sector against the governor's assistant. Students took the lead in the fight. They charged the governor with balancing the budget on the students' backs and with closing the open door. There was much debate about what sector of state government should receive the stiffest reduction—health, welfare, elementary and secondary education, or mental health. Higher education did not fare well. It received $93 million in new operating dollars for the 1981-83 biennium, but it gave more than $150 million through increased tuition and fees and a "draw-down" from a higher education facilities construction and maintenance fund account, for a net loss of $57 million from the 1979-81 biennium budget level.

Comparison of the Price-Setting Process in the Public and Private Sectors

To compare the tuition- and fee-setting processes at Yale and in the State of Washington, we will examine the economic contexts faced, the political processes used, and the policy issues addressed in these two settings.

Economic Context. The economic conditions facing Yale and the State of Washington were remarkably similar. They both confronted massive inflation, significant cutbacks in federal aid, and rapidly mounting energy costs. In Washington, the economic problems faced by the state and by higher education were exacerbated by the worst economic downturn since the Great Depression. These contextual factors forced both Yale and the State of Washington to raise tuition and fees significantly. The only contextual factor that served to dampen the increase was the information collected in both settings on fees charged by competing institutions.

Table 2. Existing and Recommended Tuition and Fee Levels in the State of Washington

Total Academic Year Tuition and Fees	1978-81	Council for Postsecondary Education Recommendations 1981-83	Legislative Recommendations 1981-83	Percent Increase 1978-81 to 1981-83	Fees in Seven Comparison States
Doctoral Universities					
Resident Undergraduate	$ 687	$ 896	$1,176	71%	$1,236
Nonresident Undergraduate	2,394	3,150	3,255	36	3,730
Resident Graduate	$ 771	$1,008	$1,386	79%	$1,556
Nonresident Graduate	2,736	3,600	3,879	41	4,050
Regional Universities					
Resident Undergraduate	$ 618	$ 783	$ 942	55%	$ 908
Nonresident Undergraduate	1,983	2,586	3,210	61	2,617
Community Colleges					
Resident Undergraduate	$ 306	$ 408	$ 519	69%	$ 572
Nonresident Undergraduate	1,188	1,572	2,037	71	1,234

Source: Council for Postsecondary Education, 1981.

Political Processes. The political processes differed dramatically in the two situations. At Yale, the process was closed, and only three groups played a significant role. The Corporation members—trustees—and senior officers—president, provost, and dean—derived most of their power from their structural positions within the university, while staff derived their power from the expertise that they brought to the process. At Yale, the primary base of power was the knowledge shared among the three groups, which served to render the process genteel. Although the students could have exerted significant coercive power by virtue of their ability to abandon the university structure, they chose not to do so.

In contrast, the process in Washington was more open, and it involved a larger number of groups. Because the process took place within a democratic system of government, all participants traced some portion of their power to their position in the state governmental structure. While the amount of structural power that they held varied markedly, depending on their position, many chose to take advantage of whatever power they had. Some players—Council for Postsecondary Education staff, institutional administrators, Governor's Budget Office staff, legislators who took an interest in the problem, and legislative staff with experience in tuition- and fee-setting issues—also brought a substantial amount of expertise to the table. Personality and opportunity sources of power were also available to players, although they played only a limited role in this case.

The process was initially relatively genteel, and knowledge sharing remained the primary base of power as long as the fee increases were viewed as reasonable. However, when the increases came to be seen as onerous, additional power bases were exercised. The groups representing the institutions—students, faculty, and administrators—united to oppose the increase at the 1981 legislative session, using normative power and such symbolic phrases as *balancing the state budget on the backs of students* and *closing the open college door in Washington* to advance their position. Students went even further, exercising their power in a coercive fashion by threatening to drop out of school.

Policy Issues. Both at Yale and in Washington, the primary policy issue was the competing claims of price (or access) and quality. In both settings, there was genuine concern about the burden that tuition and fee increases would pose for students and their families. Staff members were asked to assess the feasibility of cutting operating budgets so as to reduce that burden. In both cases, analysis showed that reductions were possible but that they could not go beyond a certain level without compromising quality. Thus, the budget-reduction option had limited utility in this situation, and it did not obviate the need for increases in tuition and fees. In Washington the resulting increases led to a dramatic change in policy on access to higher education. Washington had a long tradition of open access at all levels of higher education. The increases brought the state much closer to the national average for tuition and fees at all levels of higher education.

Washington also faced the policy issue of deciding what portion of the state budget should go to higher education. Higher education's portion of the state budget had steadily declined over the preceding decade. That trend continued in the 1981–83 biennium, with prisons and social and health services programs getting the lion's share of new resources. This trend to a decreasing budget share for higher education exists in most states, to the great concern of higher educators.

Conclusion

In this chapter, we have examined the politics of price setting in two quite different higher education settings. The similarities and the differences are striking, but they are not unexpected.

One problem that these two case studies highlight is the absence among participants of a clear understanding of marketing concepts and of their applicability to the problem of tuition and fee setting. The primary impetus for changes in price and the budget levels ultimately set had more to do with major economic and political forces and with the needs of the institutions concerned than they did with a clear understanding of what the market—that is, what students and their parents—could and should bear. This conclusion is essentially the same as that drawn by Rusk and Leslie (1978) in their study of tuition-setting practices in public higher education. Clearly, such an understanding could make price setting better informed and perhaps more humane, and it would leave those who make the tuition and fee decisions less exposed to the vagaries of outside economic and political forces.

References

Bacharach, S. B., and Lawler, E. J. *Power and Politics in Organizations: The Social Psychology of Conflict, Coalitions, and Bargaining.* San Francisco: Jossey-Bass, 1980.

Council for Postsecondary Education. *Summary of Legislative Action.* Olympia: Council for Postsecondary Education, State of Washington, 1981.

March, J. G., and Simon, H. A. *Organizations.* New York: Wiley, 1958.

Rusk, J. J., and Leslie, L. L. "The Setting of Tuition in Public Higher Education." *Journal of Higher Education,* 1978, *49* (6), 531–547.

Strauss, G. "Some Notes on Power Equalization." In H. J. Leavitt (Ed.), *The Social Science of Organizations: Four Perspectives.* Englewood Cliffs, N.J.: Prentice-Hall, 1963.

Suttle, J. L. "The Rising Costs of Private Higher Education." *Research in Higher Education,* 1983, *18* (3), 253–270.

Tonn, J. C. "Political Behavior in Higher Education Budgeting." In S. S. Micek (Ed.), *Integrating Academic Planning and Budgeting in a Rapidly Changing Environment: Process and Technical Issues.* Boulder, Colo.: National Center for Higher Education Management Systems, 1980.

Vroom, V. H. "A New Look at Managerial Decision Making." In H. L. Tosi and W. C. Hamner (Eds.), *Organizational Behavior and Management: A Contingency Approach.* (Rev. ed.) Chicago: St. Clair Press, 1977.

Yale University. "Paying for a Yale Education: Report of the Provost's Task Force on Trends and Prospects in Tuition, Enrollment, and Student Aid." New Haven, Conn.: Yale University, 1982.

Joseph E. Gilmour, Jr., is executive assistant to the chancellor at the University of Maryland at College Park.

J. Lloyd Suttle is dean of administrative affairs and acting dean of student affairs, Yale College.

Assessing the impact of pricing in higher education is complicated by widespread price discounting. Both student aid programs and tax policy can reduce the actual costs paid by students and their families.

Reducing the Burden of Price

Janet S. Hansen

Setting prices for undergraduate education and assessing the effects of those prices on consumers and institutions are complex and difficult tasks, as earlier chapters in this volume have shown. The difficulty is compounded by the fact that only some students at any given institution actually pay the price stated in the catalogue for tuition and fees. Others pay a variety of lower prices, thanks to the efforts of private donors, governments, and the college itself. Some students receive outright grants to reduce the net price that they must pay. Some students benefit from a variety of subsidized or market-rate credit mechanisms that reduce the immediate burden of paying for college and, in the case of subsidized loans, that reduce its net price as well. In addition, the financial burden of college costs can be lowered by programs of student employment and by incentives encouraging advance savings. This chapter examines these devices for reducing the burden of price on consumers of higher education.

Price reductions and subsidies are not new in higher education. William G. Bowen (1983), president of Princeton University, cites the existence of a Fund for Pious Youth that gave financial assistance to needy students as early as 1759. Such discounts have become widespread and highly visible in the last twenty-five years, because governments have made them increasingly possible. Most price discounting, credit extension, and subsidized employment are accomplished through so-called student financial aid programs. However, student aid is not the only way of reducing the burden of prices for students and families. Government tax policy can also have this effect, and it will be discussed in the next-to-last section.

L. H. Litten (Ed.). *Issues in Pricing Undergraduate Education.*
New Directions for Institutional Research, no. 42. San Francisco: Jossey-Bass, June 1984.

Student Financial Aid

In the 1982-83 academic year, price discounts in the form of student financial aid reached a level of about $16 billion, much of it directed to undergraduates. In nominal terms, this marks an astonishing growth over a twenty-year period; in 1963-64, such aid amounted to about $550 million. Even in real terms—that is, taking inflation into account—student aid grew during that period by about nine times.

History. As already noted, student aid goes back to the earliest days of higher education in this country. For most of our history, however, such aid primarily took the form of scholarships, which recognized academic merit or performance as well as (sometimes, instead of) financial need. Colleges themselves provided the funds for most of these discounts, usually from money raised from alumni and other donors.

Government is a relative latecomer to the provision of direct financial aid to college students, although the states traditionally provided indirect aid by subsidizing public higher education and by charging low prices at state colleges and universities. New York established a scholarship program in 1913, but few states followed suit until the 1960s. The federal government gave a small amount of financial aid during the Depression in the form of loans and work opportunities, but it did not become involved in a major way until after World War II. The postwar Veterans Readjustment Act, more commonly known as the G.I. Bill, provided billions of dollars in education assistance, but it was not meant primarily to provide student aid. Rather, it was intended to ease the transition of servicemen back into civilian life and to prevent labor markets from being flooded. Nevertheless, it became an important precedent, because it proved that the federal government could aid large numbers of students in a major way without serious negative consequences for higher education.

Although there were a number of attempts to involve the federal government in student aid in the 1940s and 1950s, it took the shock of Sputnik to produce the first federal program designed explicitly for this purpose, the National Defense Education Act loan program of 1958. The War on Poverty of the 1960s and rising concern about the equality of educational opportunity caused student assistance programs to take off. The federal government created four major programs between 1964 and 1972, and by the early 1970s more than half of the states were also providing direct assistance to students.

Sources. From its start as a mostly college-based effort, student aid has become a partnership among institutions and state and federal governments. In recent years, the federal government has become the overwhelmingly dominant partner. For 1982-83, Congress appropriated about $9 billion for student aid programs, which served to make about $12 billion actually available to students. (Available funds exceed appropriated dollars because federal loan subsidies generate more loan dollars than they cost. In addition, some federal programs require matching money from institutions of higher education or other sources, such as employers of students who participate in work programs.) All states had some kind of need-based grant programs, under which about $1 billion was awarded. Some states also had nonneed-based grant programs, under which another $100 million was distributed. Colleges themselves provided more than $2 billion in student aid, either from past and current gifts or from funds set aside from current revenues. Finally, a host of other donors, such as local service clubs, awarded scholarships, usually of a few hundred dollars each, to college students. Employers, too, sometimes paid the educational expenses of their employees.

Forms of Student Aid. Student aid traditionally takes three basic forms: outright discounts (grants or scholarships), credit (subsidized or unsubsidized loans), and work opportunities. The federal government, the biggest source of student aid, has programs of all three types. The Pell Grant program, created in 1972, provides need-based grants of up to $1,800 to all eligible undergraduates. Students apply directly to the government for these funds. Under the three so-called campus-based programs—Supplemental Educational Opportunity Grants, created in 1965; National Direct Student Loans, today's version of the 1958 program; and College Work-Study, created in 1964—institutions receive federal funds to make grants and low-interest (now 5 percent) loans and to provide students selected according to federal eligibility standards with jobs. Finally, students whose family income does not exceed $30,000 annually or who can qualify on the basis of financial need can borrow up to $2,500 a year from banks and other lenders under the federally subsidized Guaranteed Student Loan (GSL) Program created in 1965. The federal government guarantees these loans against default, pays the interest while borrowers remain in school, and pays lenders a special allowance to supplement the below-market interest rate of 7 to 9 percent paid by borrowers. In addition to these programs aimed directly at students, the federal government also makes educational benefits available to eligible individuals under the G.I. bill and Social Security, and makes unsubsidized but federal guaranteed loans to parents at below-market interest rates (now 12 percent) under a program called Parent Loans for Undergraduate Students (PLUS).

Not only have student aid programs grown dramatically over the past two decades, but the balance among types of aid has begun to shift from grants to loans. Gillespie and Carlson (in press) estimate that in 1970-71 grants accounted for about two thirds of all aid to students; loans accounted for 28 percent, and work for 5 percent. In 1982-83, the loan share had grown to 44 percent, while grants had shrunk to 53 percent, and work to 4 percent. This shift from grants to loans has major policy implications that will be explored in the next two sections.

Recent Developments

On taking office in 1981, President Reagan made student aid one target of his efforts to reduce the size of the federal budget. He proposed cuts of as much as 40 percent in some programs and outright elimination of others. He also proposed limiting eligibility. For example, graduate students would have been removed from the Guaranteed Student Loan Program altogether, and all undergraduates would have had to qualify under a financial needs test. Although Congress eventually declined to make these cuts, and student aid has emerged from the budget wars of the past two years relatively unscarred, the Reagan proposals were momentous for higher education. In the first place, they signaled an end to the rapid increases in financial aid of the 1970s. Even though large cuts have not been made, the programs are no longer growing fast enough to keep pace with rising costs, so they are worth less in real terms every year. In the second place, higher education realized with a jolt how important federal student aid had become in college financing. A scramble to identify possible alternatives and supplements to federal assistance began.

With federal funds threatened and with both state and institutional budgets under pressure, the possibilities of expanding such relatively expensive forms of aid as grants and employment subsidies were limited. Nevertheless, a number of colleges stepped up fund raising for student aid. For example, Cornell created an innovative work program supported by alumni contributions. A number of states began to explore the creation of state versions of college work-study, and some states increased their grant appropriations. By far the most attention, however, has focused on new forms of credit and sources of loan funds as a way of maintaining open access to higher education. Such institutions as Vanderbilt, Hood, and Dickinson announced that they would use some of their endowment to make loans to students. Others, such as Macalester, arranged with banks to provide students with assured access to loans. Some colleges initiated special fund-raising drives among alumni to raise loan capital, and others talked of approaching businesses and foundations for help. Washington University and others initiated prepayment plans, under which families could prepay four years of tuition, thereby locking in current tuition levels. Often, these plans were combined with loans that gave parents the cash for prepayment and tax deductions for interest charges.

Most attention, however, centered on a plan first proposed in Illinois—to use tax-exempt bonds to raise money that institutions could lend to students and parents outside the framework of the federal Guaranteed Student Loan Program. States that adopted this approach set up new loan authorities or extended the authority of existing agencies to issue bonds on behalf of single institutions or groups of institutions. To date, several states have passed enabling legislation, and a handful of schools, including Northwestern University, Rush Medical College, Colby College, Dartmouth College, and a consortium of nine Massachusetts colleges, have raised loan capital in this way.

Perhaps the major lesson of the recent search for creative new financing solutions to the problem of student aid is that the federal government remains an almost indispensable partner in most cases. Few observers believe that new programs can replace any significant part of the nearly $8 billion in loan capital provided by GSL in 1981. In other words, new or alternative programs can only supplement, not replace, federal programs. Many colleges do not have the financial strength to raise money in bond markets, and in any case programs like those being established with tax-exempt bond revenues may be more appropriate for graduate than for undergraduate students. Moreover, Congress is already wary of the volume of tax-exempt bonds being issued by states and other authorities for both educational and other purposes, and it periodically considers clamping down to curb tax revenue losses.

Another lesson from recent events is that existing federal programs probably have more potential than has been realized. Many institutions discovered that a number of families mistakenly thought they had lost their eligibility for guaranteed student loans when income limits were reimposed in 1981; actually, they could still qualify. Though GSL volume dropped by 20 percent in 1981-82, it grew by nearly 25 percent in 1982-83. Futhermore, the new PLUS program, an adjunct of GSL adopted in 1980 and just getting under way as other funds were endangered by recent cuts, provided parents with a new (though less highly subsidized) source of loan funds that are available without regard for family income.

Although the crisis in student aid funding that loomed in 1981 and 1982 has abated, the need to explore creative financing options for the future has not passed. Political pressure on Congress to restrict guaranteed student loans diminished as interest rates (and therefore the costs of federal subsidies) fell, but it could rise again if interest rates head back up. If and when Congress and the administration decide to tackle the problem of reducing federal budget deficits that approach $200 billion a year, all federal spending programs could be vulnerable. At the minimum, it seems unlikely that significant amounts of new federal dollars will flow into student aid. This means that current levels of funding will provide increasingly less real help as college costs continue to rise.

Issues in Student Financial Aid

For thirty years, beginning roughly with the founding of the College Scholarship Service (CSS) in 1954, a remarkable consensus has existed about how price discounts should be distributed to students through the financial aid system. The colleges that banded together to form CSS agreed that colleges should not bid against each other for students and that aid should be awarded on the basis of financial need. Some contradictory practices—grants-in-aid to athletes, merit awards to exceptional scholars—persisted, but for the most part undergraduate financial aid was characterized at the institutional level by the principle of using available funds to make need-based awards. When state and federal governments got into the act, they, too, adopted these principles. Almost all student aid was designed to promote access to, and to a less extent choice among, institutions of postsecondary education.

The consensus still holds for the most part, although it is beginning to fray. Questions that have not been heard in the student aid arena for the past quarter century are now being raised. These questions are being generated by such forces as uncertainty about what large expenditures on student aid have accomplished and by the increasing competition among colleges for students as the much-heralded baby bust of the 1980s arrives. Some of the answers will involve political and philosophical judgments rather than analyses of fact. Others are more or less amenable to research, but much remains to be done. An overview of the major issues follows.

How Heavy Is the Burden of College Costs? Steep annual increases in tuition levels and annual total costs of $12,000 or more at a handful of highly visible colleges have contributed to the widespread impression that the costs of college have become increasingly burdensome. Much was heard during the 1970s about the need of middle-income as well as of poor families for government help in meeting such costs. One result was the passage of the Middle-Income Student Assistance Act in 1978 (MISAA), which extended eligibility for the Pell Grant program to additional groups of students and which removed the income ceiling for Guaranteed Student Loans. In contrast, the Reagan administration has justified its proposals for cutting back student aid programs by suggesting that parents must bear the primary responsibility for their children's college expenses and by the claim that government assistance had relieved parents who could afford to pay of their responsibilities.

In their study of trends in student aid, Gillespie and Carlson (in press) demonstrate that over the past twenty years college costs have risen at a slightly lower rate than disposable personal income per capita. However, such findings are not likely to end the discussion about the burdens of educational costs. For one thing, there is evidence that the situation has reversed in the past several years and that stagnating incomes during the economic recession failed to keep pace with inflation-driven costs. Moreover, observers have noted that, even if costs do not rise faster than income, they still represent a large portion of most families' annual disposable earnings, and they can therefore seem burdensome, even though families are expected to use savings and other assets as well as current income to pay college costs. Finally, education has to compete against an ever-widening array of consumer goods and services for the family's disposable earnings.

The question of the burden of college costs is complicated by the fact that the nature of the student body has changed over the past several decades. Higher education in America has changed from an elite to a mass phenomenon, and families from all parts of the financial spectrum aspire to higher education for their children. In addition, students are becoming increasingly older, and many are enrolled part-time. Older and part-time students both pose complicated problems for the student financial aid system, which originally focused on traditional students. The system has coped less easily with such issues as defining students as financially independent of their parents for aid purposes and calculating need accurately for students who live in the community rather than in college dorms and who often have families to support.

Finally, there is the question of whether parents are willing to pay for higher education for their children. Some research suggests that parents may be unwilling to pay what need-analysis services and others say they should pay, and other studies show that many students have high levels of unmet need; that is, their costs exceed the resources that they are calculated to have available for college. Nevertheless, these students are enrolled in college, which suggests that, despite findings of unmet need, they are indeed managing to meet their expenses. Such contradictory findings underscore the difficulties that both analysts and policy makers face when they try to decide how burdensome college costs are and for whom.

What Has Student Aid Accomplished? Now that student aid has reached the multibillion-dollar level, it is not surprising that questions about what this aid has accomplished are frequent. For the last several decades, promotion of educational equality has been the raison d'etre of government efforts, so attempts to gauge the success of aid programs usually focus on the extent to which educational opportunity has in fact been equalized.

In a monograph prepared for the National Institute of Education, Hansen (1982) argued that student aid has had no demonstrable effect on participation in higher education. His study has been severely criticized on methodological grounds, and it has been contradicted by at least two other pieces of research. Manski and Wise (1983) have concluded that the Pell Grant program has had a positive effect on college enrollments, especially in community colleges, while work done for the National Commission on Student Financial Assistance by Lee and colleagues (Applied Systems Institute, Inc., 1983) also suggests that student aid has made a difference in who attends college. Both studies are not without problems. Manski and Wise base their conclusions on extrapolations from the National Longitudinal Study of the high school class of 1972, a class that for the most part entered college before the big boom in federal assistance. Lee's conclusions are necessarily impressionistic; they depend on data sources that, while the best available, do not describe all students in higher education.

Assessing the effects of student aid programs presents researchers with substantial problems, many of which remain to be solved. Even what constitutes an effect is at issue: Should one look at enrollment rates, or at persistence or graduation rates, or at some other measure? How can one deal with counterfactual possibilities; for example, the question of what would have happened to enrollment rates if there had been no student aid?

There are other conceptual difficulties in attempts to assess the results of student aid. For example, Hansen (1982) assumes that government subsidies have been targeted to low-income students, and he therefore looks for results that suggest improvements in the enrollment rates of such students relative to better-off but less-subsidized peers. However, it is not clear that the subsidies have in fact been as targeted as Hansen indicates. The next section of this chapter will suggest that the existence of indirect subsidies through the tax system shifts the incidence of subsidy somewhat, because tax subsidies tend to benefit families with above-average incomes. Even within the student aid system, elimination of the GSL income ceiling in 1978, coupled with historically high interest rates, has shifted student aid subsidies toward loans and away from grants, and loan recipients include a much larger proportion of middle- and upper-income students. Reimposition of an income ceiling for student loans in 1981 has changed this situation somewhat, but it still confounds analysis that covers recent years.

Another difficulty is that student aid should probably be considered a necessary but not a sufficient condition for the fostering of educational opportunity. Other conditions over the last decade have not been as positive as the growth in aid funds. Perhaps the most important is that the quality of schooling is often poor, especially in cities where many low-income families reside. Many disadvantaged students have not received the kind of education in the lower schools that makes higher education a realistic possibility.

In a system where student aid makes the stated price of higher education and its actual price quite different for many families, the absence of information is a barrier that limits the effectiveness of aid programs. Students make academic choices that influence their chances of pursuing various kinds of higher education in the ninth grade or earlier, yet most families have little way of knowing what college will cost until the student nears the end of his or her high school years, when financial aid is awarded. It is probably impossible to make any final judgments about the effectiveness of student aid in changing student behavior until better information is available at the time when students must make these critical academic choices.

Despite the difficulties, however, it will be increasingly important to address the issue of what student aid has accomplished. Aid programs suffered remarkably little criticism for many years, but this is no longer the case. Some policy makers can be heard to argue that they have made no difference; others voice the somewhat contradictory position that student aid has encouraged too many students to go to college, including many who should not have gone at all; that it has discouraged saving for college; and that is has contributed to the decline in academic standards that is now being perceived at all levels of education. Thus, the effectiveness of student aid is a fertile issue for additional work.

Who Should Get Price Discounts? As student aid programs have become large and visible, the issue of who should benefit has become urgent. As often happens with programs targeted to a restricted group, there has been pressure to expand financial aid eligibility to an increasing proportion of the student body. Where the dominant federal programs are concerned, these pressures culminated in the Middle-Income Student Assistance Act (MISAA) of 1978, described earlier. As a result, GSL costs soared, both because the number of borrowers increased and because interest rates were rising, which greatly increased federal obligations for special allowance payments that supplement the low fixed interest rate on such loans. MISAA was hardly in place before the budget crunch of the early 1980s led the federal government to retrench. In 1981, Congress rescinded some of MISAA's provisions, most notably by reimposing an income ceiling of $30,000 for Guaranteed Student Loans, with exceptions for families making more than $30,000 who could demonstrate financial need.

With prospects for increases in federal aid dim, the question of how narrowly to target existing funds becomes critical. There is a danger that benefits to low-income students, the original target of most student aid, will be seriously diluted if too many students must share a stable or shrinking pool of assistance. Research and analysis are needed on the extent to which such dilution may already have occurred and on the benefits, drawbacks, and probable effects of Reagan administration proposals to retarget student aid on the neediest.

A growing debate about who should benefit from student assistance focuses on the shorthand expression: *Need versus Merit*. This debate goes to the heart of the existing consensus about the central role of family financial conditions in the award of student aid. It is likely to be one of the hotter and more passionately argued pricing issues in the foreseeable future.

To some extent, a backlash against the domination of need-based aid began in the 1970s, fueled by some of the same forces that led to MISAA. Student aid, often thought of popularly as "scholarships," still carries strong connotations of merit and reward for achievement. Parents, especially middle-income parents who qualified for little or no need-based financial assistance but who felt the burden of college costs, sometimes complained that aid went to mediocre students while their own high-achieving children received nothing. In fact, the tension between need-based and merit-based discounting has never been absent from the student aid arena, and merit-based awards have persisted during the past three decades when need-based aid predominated. Responding to the traditional appeal of rewards for academic merit, the Reagan administration has considered launching a new federal initiative to encourage such awards.

The circumstance that seems sure to bring the tension over the relative claims of merit to new levels in the 1980s is the so-called baby bust. With the number of young people of traditional college age declining precipitously in the 1980s and 1990s, there are widespread fears that colleges will increasingly use price discounts to attract students in the battle for survival. In fact, there are frequent allegations that price competition is already under way. Such competition raises a number of concerns. One major concern is that the costs of engaging in bidding wars for talented students will cut into aid available for financially needy students and that access to higher education will therefore suffer. Another is that only the financially strong colleges can survive such bidding wars and that the financial strength of all institutions will be sapped. These issues deserve careful analysis. So do the questions of whether merit-based aid is likely to affect either the college-going decisions or the college choices of recipients and whether increasing the emphasis on merit in student aid will indeed promote educational excellence.

Finally, the need-based aid consensus of recent decades may also be challenged by rising concerns over national manpower needs and the possibility that aid could be linked to study in critical fields. Already, recognition that there are severe shortages of high school mathematics and science teachers has produced numerous proposals for financial incentives for students who enter these fields who are willing to commit themselves to teaching for a specified period of time. While the possibility of linking financial aid to manpower needs is increasingly being discussed, the debate is taking place largely without good analysis of the extent to which such incentives are likely to work and of their other probable positive and negative effects.

What Form Should Price Discounts Take? The last crucial issue in student aid is the form that price discounts should take. Should aid be given as outright grant assistance, or should it be distributed through such self-help mechanisms as loans or subsidized jobs? Is the need for help in reducing the burden of price a need for current subsidies to pay part of the price or is it a need for mechanisms that spread the payment burden over a period after the college-going years?

Philosophical issues aside, fiscal realities—loans generally are cheaper than grants—have caused loan financing of higher education to explode in recent years. The consequences of this shift in the burden of paying for college from the current generation (parents and taxpayers who provide gifts and grants) to the future generation (students who bear the obligation to repay loans) are largely unknown. Many observers are increasingly concerned about the debt burdens that students are assuming and about the implications of these debts for career and marriage decisions and for the ability of borrowers to undertake other kinds of loans, for example, for cars and homes. Research is needed on these implications as well as on how students and parents perceive and decide about the costs and benefits of borrowing to pay college costs.

Another issue in the loan area involves the extent to which student loans need to be subsidized. The major student loan program, GSL, was not originally meant to be subsidized heavily but rather to provide access to capital for middle-income families. As interest rates in the general economy rose, however, the federal government created and then expanded a special allowance that it paid to lenders so that the nominal borrowing rate (now 8 percent) could be kept relatively low. In addition, the federal government has always made interest payments for students while they remained in school. The result is that federal subsidies for loans represented more than one third of all federal expenditures on student aid in 1982–83. The National Commission on Student Financial Assistance (1983) estimates that loan subsidies amounted to between 47 and 59 cents for each dollar borrowed under GSL in 1982.

Although information on who borrows under GSL is relatively poor, it is clear that GSL subsidies dilute the targeting of assistance to low-income students that characterizes other federal aid programs. Moreover, loan subsidies awarded (as they are now) on the basis of parental incomes strike many observers as misplaced, since the real need for subsidy may be more appropriately linked with the student borrower's future earnings. As federal resources become more scarce and as competition for these resources increases, loan subsidies become more open to question. At the same time, the increasing use of loans to reduce the immediate burden of paying for college underlines the importance of maintaining access to capital and of making it even easier to obtain. A number of ideas for such things as tuition advance funds, income-contingent loans, national loan banks, and new market financing mechanisms will be hotly debated in the next few years as discussions about the place and form of borrowing in postsecondary finance continue.

Finally, concern about the proper form of price discounts is likely to focus attention on student job opportunities once again. Programs to help students work their way through college have historically appealed to liberal and conservative lawmakers alike. The Reagan administration has proposed large increases for the federal College Work-Study Program, which subsidizes part-time student employment. Several congressmen have considered expanding federal encouragement of cooperative education programs, under which students combine periods of education with periods of work in jobs related to their academic interests. Policy makers debating these issues could benefit from analyses of the extent to which students are already working and from analyses of the implications of new or expanded job opportunities on the time available for academic pursuits, on the extent to which the ability of college graduates to find jobs is enhanced by pregraduation work experience, and on the extent to which the educational experiences of students are enriched or diluted by time spent on the job.

Tax Policy

In a paper prepared for the College Board, Hauptman (in press) explores existing and proposed tax policies that have the effect of reducing the burden of price for those paying for higher education. Some existing policies ease the burden by reducing taxable income. These policies include the provision that allows parents to claim children past age eighteen as dependents if they are full-time students, the exclusion of scholarship and fellowship assistance from taxable income, tax deductions for interest paid on student loans, and the exclusion from taxable income of job-related educational assistance received from employers. Other tax provisions treat income favorably when it is transferred from parents to children and provide families with ways of reducing educational expenses by giving gifts to their children or by setting up tax-favored trusts.

Hauptman estimates that current tax breaks that help to finance college expenses cost the federal government about $1.9 billion in lost revenue in fiscal year 1982. While this figure is small compared with the level of direct student aid subsidies, the tax breaks are not inconsequential. Moreover, tax breaks tend to favor families with above-average incomes, and their existence tends to counterbalance the equalizing effect of targeting student aid monies to lower-income groups.

Hauptman notes that, as budgetary pressures on such direct subsidy programs as student aid have increased, interest has grown in the kind of off-budget, indirect subsidies typified by tax policy. Three new kinds of tax breaks that would reduce the burden of higher education costs are being discussed: tuition tax credits, tax deductions for saving for college, and tax-free income on college saving accounts.

A recent Supreme Court decision (*Mueller* v. *Allen,* 1983) upholding tuition tax credits in the state of Minnesota is sure to reignite efforts to enact such credits at both the state and federal levels. In a handful of other states, tax codes already have provisions for tax credits or deductions for educational expenses. Congress has passed a tuition tax credit bill half a dozen times over the past twenty years, although such measures have never successfully negotiated the entire legislative process.

The popularity in recent years of individual retirement accounts (IRAs) has led to calls for the creation of a similar mechanism that would allow parents to save for college expenses. Under an IRA-type arrangement, parents could put a limited amount each year into a college savings account, and both the initial deposit and the income that it earned would be tax-free until they were withdrawn. One variant on this idea places the ultimate tax liability on the student beneficiary, whose tax bracket is presumably lower than that of his parents. In an effort to move in this direction while keeping losses to the federal treasury to a minimum, President Reagan proposed in 1982 to create college savings accounts in which earnings, but not the original deposits, would be tax-free. This idea was not received well in Congress, in part because it provided little real benefit above what parents can already receive through such devices as setting up savings accounts in their children's names.

Hauptman points out a number of problems that plague most proposals for new tax breaks. Often costs are difficult to determine, and they can vary enormously with the specific details envisioned, for example, whether a tax credit is limited to $500 or to $1,000 and whether it is refundable to those with low tax liability. Unless a tax break like deductions for college savings accounts is restricted in some way, as by the income ceiling that President Reagan proposed in his plan, many people who would have saved money for college anyway will save tax dollars as well. In other words, the program is more costly than it needs to be to induce additional parents to save. However, if the benefit is restricted to parents with incomes below some level like $40,000 questions arise as to how many families actually will be able to set aside money for savings in order to capture the tax benefit. In any event, the current state of federal government finances makes it highly unlikely that new tax breaks will be enacted in the near future.

Conclusion

Price discounts in higher education are varied and common. They complicate enormously the task of assessing the burden of price and of determining whether the efforts to reduce this burden should be public or private. The fact that some discounts—for example, many tax breaks—are relatively indirect and invisible only increases the difficulty. So does the fact that the goals sought by those who offer price discounts appear to be multiplying. Nevertheless, it is becoming increasingly important for analysts and policy makers to address these issues. Higher education is well into its crucial decade, when demographic swings threaten large enrollment declines and student bodies may be composed of more minority and historically disadvantaged groups than ever before. Unfortunately for colleges, these changes are occurring at a time when state and federal governments are in their worst fiscal shape in years, and the economy is pulling out of a severe recession in a recovery whose duration is hotly debated. Resources to meet the myriad needs of colleges and students are limited, and it is likely that they will remain so. Using resources equitably and efficiently is becoming increasingly important. Understanding the nature, extent, and effects of price discounts is crucial to this goal.

References

Applied Systems Institute, Inc. "Changes in College Participation Rates and Student Financial Assistance 1969, 1974, 1981." Paper prepared for the National Commission on Student Financial Assistance, 1983.
Bowen, W. G. *Maintaining Opportunity: Undergraduate Financial Aid at Princeton.* Report of the President, April 1983. Princeton, N.J.: Princeton University, 1983.
Gillespie, D. A., and Carlson, N. *Trends in Student Aid.* Washington, D.C.: The College Board, in press.
Hansen, W. L. "Economic Growth and Equal Opportunity: Conflicting or Complementary Goals in Higher Education?" Paper prepared for the National Institute of Education, 1982.
Hauptman, A. M. *Tax Breaks for College: Current and Proposed Tax Provisions That Assist Families in Financing College Costs.* Washington, D.C.: The College Board, in press.
Manski, C. F., and Wise, D. A. *College Choice in America.* Cambridge, Mass.: Harvard University Press, 1983.
Mueller v. *Allen,* 103 S. Ct. 3062 (1983).
National Commission on Student Financial Assistance. *Access and Choice: Equitable Financing of Postsecondary Education.* Report No. 7 (draft). Washington: D.C.: National Commission on Student Financial Assistance, 1983.

Janet S. Hansen is associate director for policy analysis in the Washington, D.C., office of The College Board.

Consumers of educational services incur more than financial costs. Effective pricing strategies must also deal with the costs of time, effort, risk, and social and psychological perceptions.

Pricing in Higher Education: A Marketing Perspective

Patrick E. Murphy

For many members of the middle class, the cost of sending a son or daughter to college may have become, or at least may appear to be approaching, an almost impossible financial burden. From a marketing perspective, not only are the financial considerations of the price of a college education important, but the psychological and time costs and consumers' perceptions of the risks associated with spending four or more years to attain a degree are becoming crucial. This chapter addresses these issues.

The Nature of Price

Marketing has *exchange* as its central focus. For marketing to occur, two voluntary parties must exchange something of value. In higher education, students exchange tuition dollars, time, and effort for knowledge and competence and pay fees for housing, meals, recreational and social opportunities, and so forth. Donors to a college exchange dollars for feelings of altruism, feelings of repaying the college for previous good experiences, or for some other reason.

The practice of marketing centers on management of the marketing

L. H. Litten (Ed.). *Issues in Pricing Undergraduate Education.*
New Directions for Institutional Research, no. 42. San Francisco: Jossey-Bass, June 1984.

mix factors—product (defined broadly to include services as well as physical goods), price, place (channel of distribution), and promotion (advertising, recruiting, public relations, and other communications vehicles). The emphasis in this chapter is on the price component of the marketing mix. However, the other elements will be mentioned as they affect prices and as they relate to pricing decisions.

Some comments on the nature of services are needed. Conceptual and empirical developments in this area have lagged behind developments in the marketing of physical goods, especially of consumer packaged products. Recent authors (Lovelock, 1983; Ziethaml and others, in press) have explored services marketing in depth. Several characteristics of services need to be kept in mind when relating marketing concepts to higher education.

Four essential characteristics were noted by Ziethaml and her coauthors. First, services are intangible. In their words, "because services are performances, rather than objects, they cannot be seen, felt, tasted or touched in the same manner in which goods can be sensed" (Ziethaml and others, in press). Second, production and consumption of services are inseparable. Unlike goods, services are consumed at the point at which they are produced. A lecture on art history is consumed by students during the appointed class hour. Thus, as the consumer becomes more involved with the producer, he or she receives more benefit from the exchange; that is, interested students learn more. Third, services are heterogeneous. It is difficult to standardize services in the way that one can standardize assembly line products. Heterogeneity is an obvious hallmark of higher education, both inside and outside the individual institution. Fourth, services are perishable. The empty seat in a given course, theater performance, or airline flight cannot be saved for later sale. Therefore, the synchronization of supply and demand is a constant challenge to service marketers.

Definition. For the purposes of this chapter, price will be defined as the value of a product agreed upon by the participants in an exchange process. This value has many interpretations both for the marketer and for the consumer. For example, college administrators may feel that the value should include professors' salaries, the cost of running the physical plant, money for the endowment, and a variety of other costs. For a student paying his or her way through college, the value may seem to be restricted to the few specific faculty, facilities, and services that he or she uses directly. The effort and risk dimensions of price are also very important to consumers; they will be discussed in the next section.

Consumer's View. From the marketing viewpoint, consumers do not buy products; they buy expectations of benefits (Levitt, 1960). That is, the goal of marketing is consumer satisfaction. The consumer obtains satisfaction by paying the price for the product that delivers the satisfying benefits. From the consumer's perspective, price represents the sacrifice of personal resources required to secure the product's benefits. Thus, the consumer must answer the question, Is the product worth the price? (Hoenack [1982] discusses the benefits that accrue to society from higher education, which may be different from the private benefits considered by consumers.)

One useful way of categorizing the benefits derived from a product is provided by Maslow's (1954) hierarachy of needs. The lowest-order needs are physiological. They do not relate to the essence of higher education, but college dining facilities and housing make education possible, and eating and living arrangements can facilitate or inhibit educational outcomes. A college education satisfies the recipient's safety or security needs by increasing his or her protection against unemployment and his or her expectations for a steady stream of income throughout his or her life. The students' needs to belong can be met by being part of the student body and by the interaction that comes from it. Furthermore, an alumnus or alumna has the sense of belonging to his or her alma mater.

The fourth level of Maslow's hierarchy, esteem needs, has two parts, achievement and prestige. The benefit of gaining knowledge and skills and of having them certified relates to achievement, while students and graduates of most universities have a feeling of prestige as a result of being members of a select group. Finally, according to Maslow, the need for self-actualization is seldom achieved. However, if the U.S. Army can promote itself as a self-actualizing experience ("Be all you can be in the U.S. Army"), most colleges and universities can also claim this benefit for their students.

The student or consumer of higher education must determine whether one or some combination of these benefits (knowledge, increased purchasing power, prestige, and so forth) is worth the price of a college experience. Administrators and admissions officers must be cognizant of the specific benefits that students seek and that their school offers. Unless the consumer feels that the benefits exceed the costs, he or she will not enter into an exchange with the institution.

Marketer's View. Since the relationship between financial price and revenue is much more direct than it is for the other components of the marketing mix, it is closely scrutinized not only by those who have direct control over pricing but also by many others in the organization. It is important for those who price the product of an educational institution not to look at the final price simply as the sum of costs and overhead.

In the final analysis the administrator who sets institutional prices must understand how consumers and other decision makers within the organization view price. Consumer benefits, society's (or the state legislator's) perceptions, as well as costs should all enter into the equation that determines how to price the product that the institution offers. Eventually, the price on which the administrator decides must reconcile the diverse viewpoints.

Dimensions of Price

To understand the consumer's view of price, its two dimensions, effort and risk (Murphy and Enis, forthcoming), need to be explored. Effort can be defined as the amount of financial and physical exertion required to purchase a product. These aspects of effort can be measured objectively. Although time and money are considered the two major categories of effort, effort in higher education can be greater than their sum. For example, some students just put in time at college, while others exert great effort to attain a total educational experience. This nuance is not insignificant, but it is difficult to treat explicitly in this chapter. Risk can be defined as the consumer's subjective feeling (perception) about the price of a product. Stated another way, risk is the probability of achieving desired benefits from a product given the price that has to be paid (Litten, 1983). Risk, then, refers to whether the consumer perceives that the benefits from a product will probably outweigh its cost. Monetary and nonmonetary prices are associated with both dimensions. Figures 1A and 1B show the subcategories of these dimensions and define each term.

The effort and risk levels associated with specified products allow us to

Figure 1A. Dimensions of Pricing

	Effort	*Risk*
Monetary	Financial Price	Financial
Nonmonetary	Time — Shopping Travel Waiting Performance Monitoring	Social Psychological Physical Functional

Figure 1B. Definitions in Pricing

Financial price	Cost in dollars and cents (or relevant currency)
Financial risk	The risk that the product will not be worth the financial price
Shopping time	The time that it takes to locate and evaluate a product
Travel time	The time it takes physically to get to the product
Waiting time	The time that it takes to make the actual purchase or to receive the service
Performance time[a]	The time it takes to carry out a certain action
Monitoring time[a]	The time it takes to remember to carry out a certain action
Social risk[b]	The risk that a poor product choice may result in embarrassment before the consumer's friends or family
Psychological risk[b]	The risk that a poor product choice will harm the consumer's ego
Physical risk[b]	The risk to the consumer's safety
Functional risk[b]	The risk that the product will not perform as expected

[a] Fox, 1980.
[b] Schiffman and Kanuk, 1983.

classify them. Convenience products are low on both the effort and the risk dimensions. Fresh produce, mass transit, and a shoeshine are typical convenience products. Preference products (Holbrook and Howard, 1977) have slightly higher levels of risk and effort. Preference products include consumer packaged goods, such as beer and candy, airline service, and television programs. Shopping products are higher on both the effort and the risk dimensions. Such products as automobiles, clothing, and life insurance fall into this category. Finally, specialty products have the highest levels of both risk and effort. Exclusive products, such as fine wine, and major medical services, fall into this category.

Educational products can be categorized with the same typology. Correspondence schools are probably the only educational institutions that provide convenience products. Public primary and secondary schools offer preference products to their consumers. State-supported colleges and universities and private grade schools and high schools seem to offer shopping products to consumers. In consuming the products of these institutions, students or their parents exert reasonably high levels of effort, and in selecting one such institution over another they perceive some risk. Finally, private colleges and universities offer specialty products because the financial price is high, because the consumer must exert considerable effort to benefit, and because the risk factor is high owing to the diverse philosophical approaches of private institutions.

Administrators of educational institutions must be aware of which types of products they are offering to prospective consumers. The pricing strategies associated with shopping and specialty products will be explored later in this chapter. The implications for promotion and place (channel of distribution) must also be taken into account. For instance, Harvard, which offers a specialty product, does not need to advertise or to offer courses at locations other than Cambridge. In contrast, the University of Wisconsin-Whitewater advertises its curriculum extensively and now offers courses in the Milwaukee area, fifty miles from its campus. Clearly, this institution has realized that it offers a shopping product, not a specialty product.

Effort. The effort dimension of price shown in Figure 1A has both monetary and nonmonetary aspects. Although financial price—tuition cost—receives most of the attention given the effort dimension, it is by no means the only effort that students or contributors to a college or university must expend. The financial price for enrollment in college-level courses ranges from under $100 at some community colleges to well over $10,000 per year at the most prestigious universities. This variability has implications for consumers and for the types of markets that an institution may try to attract. Ihlanfeldt (1980) presents an excellent discussion of financial price and of the gross and net price differences between public and private institutions.

Figure 1A lists five time prices: shopping time, travel time, waiting time, performance time, and monitoring time. These time prices need to be reviewed from the perspective of higher education for the student market.

Strategies that institutions can use to reduce these prices will be discussed later in this chapter. Shopping time refers to the amount of search and evaluation that a consumer must expend to locate and evaluate a given product. Since higher education offers shopping and specialty products, it could be assumed that most students would engage in extensive search and evaluation of prospective colleges. However, we know that this is often not the case. For various reasons, ranging from lack of time or money to laziness, many students do not shop for a college. Local institutions are the direct beneficiaries of students who want to minimize the shopping time component of price.

Travel time is the amount of time that it physically takes for a student to get from his or her residence to campus. Travel time tends to restrict the market for any college or university. It can be related to both the commuter student who is only willing to drive thirty minutes or less to attend school and to the resident student who is unwilling to travel long distances to attend college. Some students want to "go away" to college without traveling so far that they can seldom see their parents and hometown friends. In a commercial marketing context, waiting time refers to what one has often to do in a retail store or when taking delivery of a product made to order or purchased by mail. In higher education, this type of time is most evident in the admissions process. If the waiting time is too long for a certain student, he or she may select a competing institution. Some schools have used the concept of "rolling admissions" to reduce waiting time. Waiting time is also an element of the registration process. Finally, many courses in smaller institutions and popular courses in larger schools quickly reach their enrollment limits, so they have to be taken in a subsequent term. These deferred courses represent a third kind of waiting time. If the resulting wait is too long, the student may enroll in another college or university where the price in waiting time is less.

Performance time refers to the time and effort that it takes to carry out a certain action (Fox, 1980). In the case of a college education, the performance time for an undergraduate degree is usually four years of full-time study. The opportunity costs associated with this time price are quite significant. Economists have long studied this issue, so it will not be examined here. From a marketing standpoint, the minimum performance time is relatively standard across institutions of higher education. However, some schools have a much better reputation than others for helping students to keep the performance time to four years.

Finally, monitoring time is the amount of time that it takes to remember to carry out a given activity (Fox, 1980). This concept seems to be most applicable to the donor market, for alumni and other donors need to be reminded to contribute to the institution.

There are other time and effort prices that consumers of higher education must pay. One such price is the time requirement to exploit one's investment. Alumni of some institutions may have to spend much more time proving themselves to employers and in social settings than alumni of Ivy League schools. It is important for those who make pricing decisions not to disregard these aspects of the price that consumers pay. Financial price is an essential component of an institution's pricing strategy, but it is not the only consideration.

Risk. Figure 1A also lists five types of risk: financial risk, social risk, psychological risk, physical risk, and functional risk. The risk price is the consumer's subjective view of the balance between a product's costs and its potential benefits. Often, the perception of risk associated with purchase of a product is more important that the objective financial and time costs. Thus, the five types of risk deserve comment.

As the name implies, financial risk refers to the buyer's perception of whether the product is worth its financial cost. Most shopping and specialty products have a relatively high financial risk. Higher education is increasing in financial risk as the price escalates and as opportunity costs mount. Even public higher education, which used to be fairly inexpensive, now carries at least a moderate degree of financial risk. The high tuition for higher education makes it high or very high in financial risk.

Social risk relates to the potential embarrassment to the consumer before his or family or peers of making a poor product choice. Higher education is high in social risk, because almost all students want their choice of a college or university to be accepted by their family and friends. In research conducted several years ago (Murphy, 1981), I found that parents and friends were the strongest influencers of college choice. The social risk stakes are even higher for students who select an out-of-state institution. On the one hand, the student may not find an acceptable set of friends at the distant school. On the other hand, his or her high school friends who attend college in state may not readmit their former friend to the group.

Psychological risk is experienced by the consumer internally. The potential damage to his or her ego from an incorrect product choice may prevent the potential consumer from purchasing a product. This price can be high for students who lack self-confidence and for students whose parents have not attended college or whose friends are not attending college.

Physical risk relates to the consumer's safety. A college is generally not thought of as high in physical risk, but some campuses are. Urban campuses can be especially high in physical risk. Therefore, parents and prospective students may perceive that the price is too high, even though they like the school and its curriculum.

Finally, functional risk concerns the possibility that the product will not perform as expected. Consumer products marketers must be constantly on the alert that the advertising does not oversell the product so that functional risk will be realized. In a service industry such as higher education, there is also the risk, derived from the inseparability that the consumer characteristic mentioned earlier, that the consumer will not perform will enough to realize the benefits that he or she seeks from the service. The functional risk in higher education is seldom discussed, because society takes the benefits of a degree largely for granted. However, given the high unemployment that prevails and the inability of recent graduates to acquire jobs in their chosen field, functional risk may be perceived to be high by some prospective students who have examined other post–high school options. Functional risk can also be applied on the course level. If too many students perceive that a certain instructor or course is not effective or useful, college administrators must take action to overcome this perception.

From this discussion, it should be clear that price is a multifaceted concept. Not only the financial price and the various kinds of time and effort that one must expend to acquire an education but also the consumer's perception of the various risks involved should be evaluated by college administrators in selecting a price strategy for their institution. Some of the most common pricing strategies employed by business are discussed in the next section, which also explores their implications for higher education.

Financial Pricing Strategies

Pricing strategies should be consistent with the overall objectives of the organization. For business firms, the most common objective is long-term profit maximization. Since colleges and universities are nonprofit entities, growth, survival, cost minimization, or prestige are appropriate pricing objectives. Some of the pricing strategies to be discussed here are now employed by certain institutions, but others have not been used widely.

Psychological Pricing. Although a number of alternatives fall into the category of psychological pricing, only two seem appropriate here. The first is prestige pricing. This type of pricing strategy uses the psychological phenomenon of the price-quality relationship. Research (Monroe, 1973; Monroe and Petroshius, 1981; Olson, 1977) has found that consumers associate higher prices with higher levels of quality. In higher education, this means that higher-status institutions can and should charge higher tuition. It comes as no surprise that this strategy is widely used by the most prestigious institutions — and also by some that are not so prestigious.

The second type of psychological pricing appropriate to higher education, price lining, refers to the practice of offering different products at different price levels. For instance, a single shoe company can have several price lines of shoes. In higher education, price lining seems to have been applied in at least two areas. First, the distinction between graduate and undergraduate education usually calls for charging different prices to graduate and undergraduate students. The cost of a graduate course per credit hour is invariably higher because of the quality of instruction, laboratory fees, smaller class sizes, and other resource considerations. Some institutions make a further distinction between doctoral- and master's-level courses. These institutions may have three price lines. (Of course there are also other price differences attached to these "lines" such as prior preparation.)

Like managers in the commercial sector, educational administrators who determine price lines must be careful not to set them too close together or too far apart. Furthermore, the price differential should reflect some real degree of difference. If both undergraduate and master's-level students can enroll in the same class but different prices are charged, the institution may have a hard time justifying its policy.

Another price lining consideration for colleges and universities is raised by the distinction between full-time and part-time attendance. Part-time students are commonly charged only a flat rate per credit for the limited number of hours in which they enroll. The use of an unbundled price structure seems to be the most equitable way of dealing with these students (O'Neill, 1978). Full-time students must pay a higher rate, because the institution provides them with additional services beyond course instruction. If colleges and universities hope to increase the number of nontraditional students, a thorough review of the pricing for part-time students will be necessary. Past consumer decision rules are not apt to be adequate for pricing the institution's curricular offerings for new part-time students.

Multiple Pricing. The multiple pricing strategy relates to the decision to charge a single price or a variable price for a given product. In our mass merchandise and self-service society, almost every convenience and preference product and some shopping products have a single price. The consumer cannot negotiate. In higher education, there is a "list" or published price, but in actuality the price is variable. The most common adjustment to list price comes in the form of the financial aid that the student receives. Tierney (1980) has taken an in-depth look at financial aid. Chapman (1979), who found that the two major influences on college choice are financial price and quality, concluded (p. 55): "Clearly, since money does matter, colleges had better be thoughtful with regard to allocating grants and scholarships to prospective students, since these pricing decisions have a large impact on how students seem to choose among colleges." Therefore, it seems that this variable pricing strategy warrants the attention that it already receives on most college campuses.

Other variable prices that institutions have begun to consider involve the pricing of courses offered at locations other than the campus. Should a premium or a lower price be set for such courses? Arguments can be made for both sides. If new courses are developed for the elderly, how should they be priced? Or, if older individuals enroll in existing classes, should colleges give a senior citizen discount? This area of variable pricing needs close scrutiny by the administrators who make such decisions.

Nonfinancial Pricing Strategies

Time Pricing. Pricing strategies can also be developed to address the time and effort costs of college education. Figure 2A lists the time prices and some options for deaing with them.

Figure 2A. Marketing Strategies for Reducing Time Prices

Prices	Marketing Strategy
Shopping time	Use literature and telephone calls by admissions, students, and/or alumni
	Facilitate campus visits
	Provide videotapes of campus
	Hold multiple college fairs
Travel time	Provide carpooling assistance and travel agent connections
Waiting time	Adopt rolling admissions
	Allow applicants to learn status of application by telephone
	Streamline registration process
Monitoring time	Remind donors and students who have "stopped out"

Figure 2B. Marketing Strategies for Reducing Risk Prices

Financial risk	Provide scholarships, financial aid, "satisfaction or your money back" guarantees
Social risk	Use students and alumni to recruit
	Provide good support services
Psychological risk	Stress accomplishments of past and present students
	Provide good support services
Physical risk	Stress the school's caring attitude
	Provide counseling and advising services
Functional risk	Emphasize the stature of faculty and the availability of equipment

Shopping time is an important consideration for prospective students. One way of reducing this price is to provide better, more accessible information about the school and its programs to prospective students and their parents. Making campus visits easy to arrange and carry out is another technique for overcoming the shopping time price. Once on campus, the prospective student and his or her parents should receive prompt and courteous attention, so that shopping time can be kept to a minimum.

Travel time can present a somewhat more troublesome price for many colleges and universities. For commuter students, assistance in carpooling and use of mass transit options are possible ways of reducing travel time. Resident students could be assisted in travel to and from home. An on-campus travel agent or an off-campus agency with which the institution has an ongoing relationship would offer a good method for overcoming the relatively high price of travel in some students' minds. Since travel costs continue to rise this price should not be underestimated by college administrators.

Waiting time is another price that marketing strategies can be developed to influence. The admissions office needs to provide prospective students with accurate information about the amount of time that it takes to process an application and to make a final acceptance or rejection decision. A telephone number could be given to applicants that would enable them to check on the current status of their applications. Another aspect of waiting time is the registration process. Especially for graduate and professional students, for whom time is at a premium, waiting time could be minimized by conducting registration by mail or telephone.

Performance time for a college education takes a number of years. Several strategies can be employed to make certain that performance time takes no longer than it should. First, academic advising should be easily accessible, so that students can find out exactly what courses they need to take to graduate. Second, for students who wish to complete the work early, the prerequisite courses must be offered often or in summer school. Third, students who transfer within a university to a different college or who come from another school should receive as much assistance as they need to understand the performance time requirements. Obviously, these requirements should be realistic and not excessive.

Risk Price. Figure 2B outlines strategies that can reduce the risk price associated with higher education. Besides scholarships and financial aid, a "satisfaction or your money back" guarantee could also be used to minimize financial risk. Although this technique is common in the commerical sector, it has not to my knowledge been tried in higher education. To be useful, this guarantee would have to state clearly the performance requirements for students-as-learners, and the student's performance would have to be verified. The concept is no doubt controversial, but in the highly competitive environment that most institutions face, it may not be far off.

More traditional measures can be used to minimize other types of risk. For instance, social risk can be reduced by enlisting the help of current students and alumni in the recruitment of prospective students. Alumni can provide information about the value of a degree from the institution, and the prospective student will have evidence that current students and alumni care about them and are open to including them in the "club." Psychological risk can be decreased by stressing the accomplishments of present and past students. The fact that others from similar backgrounds who attended the school are successful should help to overcome the prospective student's fear that she or he may be making a poor choice.

Physical risk has to be handled quite carefully. Campus security and safety should not be emphasized too strongly, or the prospective student will infer that they pose a major problem. A more effective approach is to stress that "we care" for our students—mentally, physically, emotionally, and spiritually, if the institution is church-affiliated.

Functional risk could be reduced by a guarantee. Past records of placement in jobs or graduate schools is another performance measure that could be effective. Ziethaml (1981) has observed that consumers see price, personnel, and physical facilities as cues of service quality. Thus, colleges and universities should pay atention to maintenance of the physical plant and invest in faculty development and training for staff members to deal with functional risk. Publicizing the stature of faculty, especially those with national reputations, can help prospective students to feel that the education offered at an institution will be a good one.

Research Agenda

Several research questions need to be answered if pricing in higher education is to be understood. First, regarding the financial price that students and parents must pay, is there an absolute price threshold (Monroe and Petroshius, 1981) beyond which prestigious private universities might price themselves out of the market? Marketers think that there is an acceptable range of prices. If a price falls outside this range, the product will not be considered. Second, what indicators of quality do students and others (donors, parents, the general public) use in selecting or discriminating among institutional alternatives? Where does price rank among these indicators? Is the price-quality relationship as strong as it has been presumed to be for private higher education? Third, what is the relative importance of the various time dimensions of price? Admissions officers and other administrators need to identify those that are most crucial for their institution. Fourth, how important are the nonfinancial types of risk in a student's decision to attend a particular institution? How does the student assess these risks? Are there minimal levels of risk that the student is willing to accept? Fifth, is it possible to measure accurately the benefits and costs that accrue to prospective students who search actively for a college to attend? Sixth, which of the marketing strategies shown in Figure 2 have institutions found to be most effective? Does the effectiveness of a strategy depend on size, funding (public or private), or some other factor? Seventh, once the student enrolls, what benefits besides classroom instruction will the student have to pay for? The notion of unbundling higher education services (O'Neill, 1978) may become more important as colleges and universities attempt to attract nontraditional students. How should institutions price unbundled services so as to satisfy the needs of these students while still treating other students equitably?

Conclusion

Pricing in higher education is serious business. Administrators must constantly wrestle with the problem of offering a high-quality educational product at a reasonable price while adequately compensating faculty and staff and spending necessary amounts on improvements. This job is complicated by the constraints placed on these decision makers by state legislatures. As this era of low or no growth for higher education proceeds, the serious matter of pricing may become grave.

This chapter has raised some important marketing considerations in the pricing of an educational product. Consumers must be monitored constantly, and their views of pricing must be taken into consideration. The nonmonetary aspects of price must also be understood, and strategies such as those analyzed here can be used to cope with them. Pricing decisions must balance many conflicting viewpoints. Decision makers in higher education must grapple with many uncertain issues to meet the challenge.

References

Chapman, R. G. "Pricing Policy and the College Choice Process." *Research in Higher Education,* 1979, *10* (1), 37-57.

Fox, K. F. "Time as a Component of Price in Social Marketing." In R. P. Bagozzi and others (Eds.), *Marketing in the 80s: Changes and Challenges.* Chicago: American Marketing Association, 1980.

Holbrook, M. B., and Howard, J. "Consumer Research on Frequently Purchased Nondurable Goods and Services: A Review." In R. Ferber (Ed.), *Synthesis of Knowledge in Consumer Behavior.* Washington, D.C.: National Science Foundation, 1977.

Ihlanfeldt, W. *Achieving Optimal Enrollment and Tuition Revenues. A Guide to Modern Methods of Market Research, Student Recruitment, and Institutional Pricing.* San Francisco: Jossey-Bass, 1980.

Levitt, T. "Marketing Myopia." *Harvard Business Review,* 1960, *38* (4), 45-56.

Litten, L. H. Personal correspondence to P. Murphy, 1983.

Lovelock, C. H. "Classifying Services to Gain Strategic Marketing Insights." *Journal of Marketing,* 1983, *47* (3), 9-20.

Maslow, A. H. *Motivation and Personality.* New York: Harper & Row, 1954.

Monroe, K. B. "Buyers' Subjective Perceptions of Price." *Journal of Marketing Research,* 1973, *10,* 70-80.

Monroe, K. B., and Petroshius, S. M. "Buyers' Perceptions of Price: An Update of the Evidence." In H. Kassarjian and T. S. Robertson (Eds.), *Perspectives in Consumer Behavior.* (3rd ed.) Glenview, Ill.: Scott, Foresman, 1981.

Murphy, P. E. "Consumer Buying Roles in College Choice: Parents' and Students' Perceptions." *College and University,* 1981, *56* (2), 140-150.

Murphy, P. E., and Enis, B. M. *Marketing: Principles and Practice.* Glenview, Ill.: Scott, Foresman, forthcoming.

Olson, J. "Pricing as an Informational Cue: Effects on Product Evaluations." In A. G. Woodside, J. N. Sheth, and P. D. Bennett (Eds.), *Consumer and Industrial Buying Behavior.* New York: Elsevier North-Holland, 1977.

O'Neill, J. P. "An Experiment in Unbundling Services for Adults." In R. K. Loring, C. LeGates, M. J. Josephs, and J. P. O'Neill, *Adapting Institutions to the Adult Learner: Experiments in Progress.* Washington, D.C.: American Association for Higher Education, 1978.

Schiffman, L. G., and Kanuk, L. L. *Consumer Behavior.* Englewood Cliffs, N.J.: Prentice-Hall, 1983.

Tierney, M. L. "The Impact of Financial Aid on Student Demand for Public/Private Higher Education." *Journal of Higher Education,* 1980, *5,* 527-545.

Ziethaml, V. A. "How Consumer Evaluation Processes Differ Between Goods and Services." In J. H. Donnelly and W. R. George (Eds.), *Marketing of Services.* Chicago: American Marketing Association, 1981.

Ziethaml, V. A., Parasuraman, A., and Berry, L. L. "Problems and Strategies in Services Marketing." *Journal of Marketing,* in press.

Patrick E. Murphy is associate professor of marketing, Marquette University, Milwaukee, Wisconsin.

Some research issues and the literature on the pricing of undergraduate education are summarized.

Advancing the Research Agenda on Undergraduate Pricing

Larry H. Litten

The authors of the preceding chapters have identified a number of research topics and they have cited some relevant works in the literature on pricing. This chapter summarizes and supplements their contributions.

Some Issues in Pricing

Throughout this volume, statements have been made that are grounded in theory or personal observation but which have not been subjected to broad, systematic research. Many of the statements that were based on empirical research drew on studies conducted under circumstances that differ from those of today or that might prevail in the future. For these reasons, there is a current research agenda, and since times and circumstances will continue to change (especially in an area where we can anticipate acute pressures and major innovations), there will always be a research agenda, relating to pricing in higher education—its nature, the processes by which it is accomplished, and its effects. In this section a substantial, though not exhaustive, list of price-related research questions is specified. Many of these questions can be addressed at a general level and such efforts will provide useful information for public policy. Since individual institutions differ in nature and operate in particular markets, many of these questions will also have to be addressed at the institutional level if the answers are to provide guidance for institutional policies.

The Overarching and Perennial Question

To what extent are current policies and practices in allocating costs (that is, charging prices and providing for payment) to various parties (students, parents, the taxable public, private philanthropy, employers, and so forth) just, effective, and efficient in producing the individual and social benefits of higher education?

More Specific (and Perhaps More Researchable) Questions

1. What conditions—institutional or environmental—have led to the use of the various pricing principles discussed by Shaman and Zemsky in Chapter One, or to combinations of these principles?

2. What are the effects (financial, marketing, political, and educational) of employing the various pricing principles?

3. To what extent have educational price increases been driven by inflation, by quality improvements, by increased individual demand, or by external subsidy systems (for example, federal aid)?

4. What values and goals characterize the behavior or perspectives of different interest groups regarding prices—faculty, administrators, trustees/regents, legislators, public bureaucracies, and students? To what degree are there convergent or conflicting interests among these groups? To what extent are there differences within these groups?

5. How have the interests of these groups and their behavior toward prices and pricesetting varied over time? What conditions lead a group to take direct political action regarding pricesetting? What political mechanisms have been used by which groups and to what effects?

6. To what extent might differential pricing by program, level of instruction, or time or place of offerings affect demand by different types of students (especially nontraditional students)? What are the institutional costs and requirements (administrative, promotional, financial aid, and so on) that are associated with such practices? How can real cost-of-production differences be separated from accidental differences (for example, seniority-related staffing patterns) or inefficiencies when effecting cost-related pricing? What time frame is appropriate when determining program costs? How are general overhead or joint costs across programs to be allocated under differentiated pricing arrangements? What balance should be adopted in differential pricing among the various bases for such differentiation (for example, costs of production, demand, competition, return on student investment)? What are the institutional political aspects of implementing differential pricing (who is affected, mobilized, with what objections or vested interests); what are the political effects of implementation (that is, realignments of power across programs with different incomes or market positions)? Will differential pricing cause students to constrain the breadth or variety of their educational experiences?

7. To what extent does the unbundling of prices for different functions lead to greater equity among users, to greater educational demand (at least among some groups), and, through increased demand, to the generation of greater aggregate educational benefits? To what extent will functional price unbundling reduce the use of services such as advising, counseling, or participation in cultural activities in ways that diminish the general quality of an educational environment and, consequently, the individual utilities available in a given institution?

8. To what extent do (should) current prices capture resources that permit educational research and development, capital improvements, and other investments that bestow future benefits? Who pays (should pay) the price for this type of educational cost?

9. To what degree do various types of students and their families consider current financial outlays versus more sophisticated present value assessments of alternative investments and various financing options when considering educational expenditures? How much do students and their families know about prices (especially net prices across different educational options), financing mechanisms, and the total costs of various forms of credit? When do they acquire this information? How accurate is it? Where does the information come from and is it being provided efficiently? How can consumers become more sophisticated and better informed regarding the prices of education and mechanisms for paying them?

10. How and to what extent do anticipated or actual debt levels affect college choices (for example, institutions and majors) and the postgraduation behavior (careers, savings, marriage, and childbearing) among various types of students?

11. How will students and their families respond to various existing and proposed financing innovations such as Clifford Trusts, Crown Loans, educational savings accounts, prepayment plans, and tuition-offsetting endowment trusts? How will such options affect family financial and educational behavior and the assumption of educational costs across generations?

12. To what degree does consumer ignorance of educational production processes and the intangibility of many educational outcomes allow for pricing practices that involve subsidies by students and their families of academic activities that do not relate to undergraduate education (for example, some research, graduate instruction, and consulting)? To what degree does consumer ignorance of educational production processes inhibit rational expenditure behavior that would restrain prices in higher education or create direct political pressure for such restraint (for example, does the use of price as a proxy for quality impede the implementation of cost-reducing and price-lowering efficiencies)?

13. What are the nonfinancial costs that students, and those who influence them, consider in college selection? What relative weight are these costs given by various types of students and at what points in the selection process

are they of concern? What information is used regarding these costs, how is it obtained, and how accurate is it?

14. How responsive are various types of students to differences in financial and nonfinancial costs? How much do price elasticities differ for different types of institutions and different specific institutions, and how much will the appropriate analytic models in this area need to differ across institutions? How do various financial and nonfinancial prices (for example, aid policies, admissions requirements) affect the character of an institution's student body (that is, the mix of students)?

Further Reading and Professional Resources

Academicians tend to use longer words than the general populace. It is not surprising, therefore, that price, a dirty word in higher education has five letters, instead of the customary four. Almost everyone in academia thinks about price; they even talk quietly about it behind ivy-covered walls, but very few people write publicly about it. Of 16,413 entries in the ERIC bibliography on higher education, 297 (1.8 percent) are indexed with tuition as a topic; only 103 (0.6 percent) have tuition as their major focus. (*Price* and *pricing* are not keywords in the ERIC indexing system.) At present, the National Association of College and University Business Officers (NACUBO) reports that it has produced no materials that deal directly with pricesetting (Brown, 1983). This is not to overlook, of course, that there is a constant flow of ink in the popular press, from *Good Housekeeping* to *Money Magazine* to the local newspaper, on the issues of rising college costs and how to pay for college.

This situation appears bound to change, however. Yanikoski and Wilson (in press) observe in their 1983 review of recent differential pricing developments that pricing in higher education is on the verge of a new era, and that principles and practices which shaped tuition strategies during decades past are now coming under increasing scrutiny. Readers who wish to prepare further for this new era and who desire to contribute to its development are encouraged to read further in a variety of literatures. A selection of such readings is listed below by topic. The most thorough and basic treatise on higher education pricing is Nerlove's (1972) article.

Selected Literature Relating to Higher Education Pricing

General Price Theory

Stigler, G. J. *Theory of Price.* New York: Macmillan, 1966.
Ward, B. *Elementary Price Theory.* New York: Free Press, 1967.

Marketing of Nonprofit Organizations: Pricing

Kotler, P. *Marketing for Nonprofit Organizations.* Englewood Cliffs, N.J.: Prentice-Hall, 1982.

Lovelock, C. H. "Theoretical Contributions from Services and Nonbusiness Marketing." In O. C. Ferrell, S. W. Brown, and C. W. Lamb (Eds.), *Conceptual and Theoretical Developments in Marketing.* Chicago: American Marketing Association, 1979.

Rados, D. L. *Marketing for Non-Profit Organizations.* Boston: Auburn House, 1981.

General Works on Tuition and Financing Undergraduate Education

Abowd, J. M. "An Econometric Model of Higher Education." In J. M. Abowd and K. Schipper (Eds.), *Managing Higher Education: Economic Perspectives.* Chicago: Center for the Management of Public and Nonprofit Enterprise, Graduate School of Business, University of Chicago, 1981.

Brown, M. K., Kahl, S., and Kriz, K. *Higher Education Indicators: Tuition, Room, and Board.* Boulder, Colo.: National Center for Higher Education Management Systems, 1981.

Carnegie Commission on Higher Education. *Higher Education: Who Pays? Who Benefits? Who Should Pay?* New York: McGraw-Hill, 1973.

Carnegie Commission on Higher Education. *Tuition: A Supplemental Statement to the Report of the Carnegie Commission on Higher Education on "Who Pays? Who Benefits? Who Should Pay?"* Berkeley, Calif.: Carnegie Commission on Higher Education, 1974.

Cohen, B. *Factors Affecting Net Tuition Revenue at Private Colleges.* Boulder, Colo.: National Center for Higher Education Management Systems, 1982.

Committee for Economic Development. *The Management and Financing of Colleges.* New York: Committee for Economic Development, 1973.

Henderson, C. *College Costs: Recent Trends, Likely Future.* Washington, D.C.: American Council on Education, 1983.

Morgan, A. W. "Cost as a Policy Issue—Lessons from the Health Care Sector." *Journal of Higher Education,* 1983, *54* (3), 280–293.

National Commission on the Financing of Postsecondary Education. *Financing Postsecondary Education in the United States.* Washington, D.C.: U.S. Government Printing Office, 1973.

Nerlove, M. "On Tuition and the Costs of Higher Education: Prolegomena to a Conceptual Framework." In T. Schultz (Ed.), *Investment in Education.* Chicago: University of Chicago Press, 1972.

O'Neill, J. *Resource Use in Higher Education.* Berkeley, Calif.: Carnegie Commismission on Higher Education, 1971.

Rusk, J. J., and Leslie, L. L. "The Setting of Tuition in Public Higher Education." *Journal of Higher Education,* 1978, *49* (6), 531–547.

Stampen, J. *Financing of Public Higher Education.* AAHE/ERIC Higher Education Research Report No. 9. Washington, D.C.: American Association for Higher Education, 1980.

Suttle, J. L. "The Rising Costs of Private Higher Education." *Research in Higher Education,* 1983, *18* (3), 253–270.

Relationships Between Prices, Demand, and Choice

Chapman, R. G. "Pricing Policy and the College Choice Process." *Research in Higher Education,* 1979, *10* (1), 37–56.

Chisolm, M., and Cohen, B. *A Review and Introduction to Higher Education Price Response Studies.* Boulder, Colo.: National Center for Higher Education Management Systems, 1982.

Litten, L. H., Sullivan, D., and Brodigan, D. L. *Applying Market Research in College Admissions.* New York: College Entrance Examination Board, 1983.

McPherson, M. "The Demand for Private Education." In C. Finn and D. Breneman (Eds.), *Public Policy and Private Higher Education.* Washington, D.C.: Brookings Institute, 1978.

Manski, C. F., and Wise, D. A. *College Choice in America.* Cambridge: Harvard University Press, 1983.

Institutional Pricing Options, Price Unbundling, Differential Pricing, Joint Production Functions

Ihlanfeldt, W. *Achieving Optimal Enrollments and Tuition Revenues: A Guide to Modern Methods of Market Research, Student Recruitment, and Institutional Pricing.* San Francisco: Jossey-Bass, 1980.

James, E. "Product Mix and Cost Disaggregation: A Reinterpretation of the Economics of Higher Education." *Journal of Human Resources,* 1981, *38,* 585–612.

James, E., and Neuberger, E. "The University Department as a Nonprofit Labor Cooperative." *Public Choice,* 1981, *36,* 585–612.

Johnson, J. C. "An Analysis of the Relationship Between Institutional Costs and Differential Tuition Levels." *Journal of Higher Education,* 1979, *50* (3), 280–288.

Lamoureux, M. E. *Marketing Continuing Education: A Study of Price Strategies.* Vancouver, B.C.: Centre for Continuing Education, University of British Columbia, 1976.

McCoy, M. *Differential Tuition at the University of Colorado.* Paper presented at the Regents' Budget Workshop, University of Colorado, August 1983.

O'Neill, J. P. "An Experiment in Unbundling Services for Adults." In R. K. Loring, C. LeGates, M. J. Josephs, and J. P. O'Neill, *Adapting Institutions to the Adult Learner: Experiments in Progress.* Washington, D.C.: American Association for Higher Education, 1978.

O'Neill, J. P. *College Financial Aid and the Employee Tuition Benefit Programs of the Fortune 500 Companies.* Princeton, N.J.: Conference University Press, 1981.

Wang, W. K. S. "The Unbundling of Higher Education." *Duke Law Journal,* 1975, *45* (1), 53–90.

Wang, W. K. S. "The Dismantling of Higher Education." *Improving College and University Teaching,* 1981a, *29* (2), 55–60.

Wang, W. K. S. "The Beginnings of Dismantling." *Improving College and University Teaching,* 1981b, *29* (3), 115–121.

Yanikoski, R. A., and Wilson, R. F. "Differential Pricing of Undergraduate Education." *Journal of Higher Education,* in press.

Financial Aid

Fenske, R. H., Huff, R. P., and Associates. *Handbook of Student Financial Aid: Programs, Procedures, and Policies.* San Francisco: Jossey-Bass, 1983.

Froomkin, J. (Ed.). *The Crisis in Higher Education.* New York: The Academy of Political Science, 1984.

Henry, J. B. *The Impact of Student Financial Aid on Institutions.* New Directions for Institutional Research, no. 25. San Francisco: Jossey-Bass, 1980.

Leslie, L. L. *Student Financing.* Boulder, Colo.: National Center for Higher Education Management Systems, 1982.

Cost Analysis

Bowen, H. *The Costs of Higher Education: How Much Do Colleges and Universities Spend Per Student and How Much Should They Spend?* San Francisco: Jossey-Bass, 1980.

Hyatt, J. A. *A Cost Accounting Handbook for Colleges and Universities.* Washington, D.C.: National Association of College and University Business Officers, 1983.

National Association of College and University Businesses Officers. *Costing for Policy Analysis.* Washington, D.C.: National Association of College and University Business Officers, 1980.

National Association of College and University Business Officers. *NACUBO Writers on Financial Management.* Washington, D.C.: National Association of College and University Business Officers, 1983.

A market research tradition is emerging within higher education, encouraged and nourished by organizations such as The College Board and the Association for Institutional Research. AIR has a special interest group for market researchers that has met at its past three annual forums; The College Board has presentations on marketing and market research at its annual meetings and has published several monographs on the topic. The National Association of College Admissions Counselors and the American Association of Collegiate Registrars and Admissions Officers have had numerous marketing presentations at their national and regional meetings and publish related articles in their journals (NACAC publishes the *National ACAC Journal;* AACRAO publishes *College and University*).

The popular press is an illuminating source of information on how the layman thinks about higher education prices. There are also some extensive discussions of college costs and of ways families and students can meet them in various handbooks devoted to aid and to more general discussions of college attendance and selection. One of the best discussions of these issues from the consumer's point of view is *How to Put Your Child Through College Without Going Broke* (New York: Research Institute of America, 1983).

Concluding Note

Pricing will continue to be central to the administration and well-being of academic institutions. The era we are entering promises many exciting initiatives in this sphere. The attendant issues offer one of the most challenging and virgin areas in which institutional researchers can invest their efforts. Because the research has been sparse to date and pricesetters have not been publishers, the existing literature on pricing is spotty. The research agenda looms large and the issues are complex. We can hope, however, that the perspectives given focus in this volume might help evoke greater attention to these perennial issues. We can also hope that this attention will produce a literature that will permit a review to be conducted five years from now that is considerably richer than this one.

Reference

Brown, D. Personal communication to L. H. Litten, 1983.

Larry H. Litten is associate director, Consortium on Financing, Higher Education, Cambridge, Massachusetts.

Index

A

Abowd, J. M., 95
American Association of Collegiate Registrars and Admissions Officers (AACRAO), 97
Applied Systems Institute, 69, 75
Appropriations, legislative: and cost-related tuition policy, 29-30; equation for, 30
Association for Institutional Research (AIR), 97
Association of American Medical Colleges, 15*n*

B

Bacharach, S. B., 48, 61
Base price: concept of, 10, 13; differentiations of, 17
Bean, J. P., 22, 33
Becker, G. S., 20, 33
Berea College, tuition lacking at, 2
Berry, L. L., 89
Bowen, H. R., 39, 44, 97
Bowen, W. G., 63, 75
Brakeley, G. A., 9, 18
Brodigan, D. L., 96
Brown, M. K., 95
Budgets: calculating base for, 49-50; corrective actions in, 50-51; and enrollment demand models, 27-30; and implementation, 51-52; in private sector, 49-52

C

California, as comparison state, 54
California, University of, financial data for, 8
Carlson, N., 65, 68, 75
Carnegie Commission on Higher Education, 95
Cash cost, concept of, 11-12, 13
Central Washington University, pricing for, 57*n*
Chapman, R. G., 85, 89, 96
Chicago, University of, financial data for, 8
Chisolm, M., 96
Clifford Trusts, 93
Cohen, B., 95, 96
Colby College, loan capital for, 66
College Board, 73, 97
College Scholarship Service (CSS), 67
College Work-Study (CWS), 11, 65, 73
Columbia University: financial data for, 8; medical school prices at, 15
Committee for Economic Development, 95
Cornell University: alumni contributions for work program at, 66; financial data for, 8; medical school prices at, 15
Costs: burden of, 68-69; cash, 11-12, 13; joint, 38; and pricing policies, 12, 14-15; unbundling of, 39-40, 85, 88
Council for Postsecondary Education (CPE), 55, 56, 57, 58, 59, 60, 61
Crown Loans, 93

D

Dartmouth College, loan capital for, 66
Deitch, K. M., 3, 6
Dickinson College, student loans from, 66
Differential pricing, and proportional cost pricing, 38-39
Discount prices: analysis of, 63-75; background on, 63; concept of, 10-11, 13; conclusion on, 75; and proportional cost pricing, 40-42; student aid as, 64-73; tax policy as, 73-75; trends in, 17; types of, 41
Donations, price of, 36

E

Eastern Washington University, pricing for, 57*n*
Educom Financial Planning Model (EFPM), 49
Effort: defined, 79-80; and marketing, 81-83

99

Ehrenberg, R. G., 25-26, 33
Elliot, W. F., 25, 26, 33
Enis, B. M., 79, 89
Enrollment: and cost-related tuition policy, 29; equations for, 21, 26-27, 32
Enrollment demand models: analysis of, 19-32; and budgets, 27-30; and enrollment forecasting, 22-23; and institutional closure, 31-32; and objective optimization, 25-27; specification and interpretation issues in, 19-22; and staffing, 31; summary on, 33; and tuition policy, 23-25; variables for, 20-21
Enrollment forecasts: and enrollment demand model, 22-23; purposes of, 28
Evergreen State College, pricing for, 57n
Externally-indexed pricing: concept of, 14, 17, 37; and productivity, 42-43

F

Faculty flow models, and enrollment demand, 31
Fenske, R. H., 97
Financial aid. *See* Student financial aid
Fox, K. F., 80n, 82, 89
Freeman, R. B., 19, 31, 33
Froomkin, J., 97

G

Gale, B. T., 3, 6
George Washington University, medical school prices at, 15
G.I. Bill, 64, 65
Gillespie, D. A., 65, 68, 75
Gilmour, J. E., Jr., 5, 47-62
Governor, pricing role of, 55-56
Guaranteed Student Loan (GSL) Program, 65, 66, 67, 68, 70-71, 72-73

H

Hansen, J. S., 5-6, 63-75
Hansen, W. L., 69, 75
Hartle, T. W., 2, 6
Harvard University: financial data for, 8; specialty product of, 81
Hauptman, A. M., 73-74, 75
Henderson, C., 95
Henry, J. B., 97

Higher education: complex pricing in, 3-4; marketing for services of, 78; and needs hierarchy, 79
Hoenack, S. A., 20, 22, 24, 25, 26, 28, 29, 30, 31, 33, 78, 89
Holbrook, M. B., 81, 89
Hood College, student loans from, 66
Hopkins, D. S. P., 27-28, 33, 35, 44
Howard, J., 81, 89
Huff, R. P., 97
Human capital model, and enrollment demand, 19-20
Hyatt, J. A., 97
Hyde, W. D., Jr., 19, 33

I

Ihlanfeldt, W., 81, 89, 96
Illinois: bonds for loans in, 66; as comparison state, 54
Illinois, University of: financial prices data for, 8; medical school prices at, 15
Indiana, as comparison state, 54
Institutions: closure of, 31-32; financial data for, in 1910, 8; price trends in, 1-2; private, pricing by, 49-54, 58-61; public, pricing for, 54-61
Interest groups, power of, 48-49

J

Jackson, G. A., 19, 33
James, E., 96
Johns Hopkins University: financial data for, 8; medical school prices at, 15
Johnson, J., 24, 33, 96
Joint costs, in proportional cost pricing, 38

K

Kahl, S., 95
Kanuk, L. L., 80n, 89
Kaufman, N. S., 34
Klavens, R., 3, 6
Kotler, P., 94
Krauth, B. M., 34
Kriz, K., 95

L

Lamoreaux, M. E., 96
Lawler, E. J., 48, 61

Lee's research, 69
Legislature: appropriations by, 29-30; pricing role of, 56
Leslie, L. L., 61, 95, 97
Levitt, T., 78, 89
Litten, L. H., 1-6, 80, 89, 91-98
Lovelock, C. H., 78, 89, 95

M

Macalester College, and student loans, 66
McCoy, M., 24, 34, 39, 44, 96
McPherson, M., 96
Mandated pricing, concept of, 14-15, 37
Manski, C. F., 27, 34, 69, 75, 96
March, J. G., 47, 61
Marketing: analysis of, 77-90; conclusion on, 88-89; consumer's view of, 78-79; and dimensions of price, 79-84; and effort, 81-83; financial pricing strategies in, 84-85; marketer's view of, 79; and nature of price, 77-79; nonfinancial pricing strategies in, 85-88; research agenda in, 88; and risk factors, 83-84; of services, 78
Maslow, A. H., 79, 89
Massachusetts, loan capital in, 66
Massy, W. F., 27-28, 33, 35, 43, 44
Medical schools, tuition and fees at, 15
Michigan, as comparison state, 54
Michigan, University of, financial data for, 8
Middle-Income Student Assistance Act (MISAA) of 1978, 68, 70-71
Minnesota: as comparison state, 54; tuition tax credits in, 74
Minnesota, University of: cost-related tuition policy at, 28-31; financial data for, 8
Monroe, K. B., 84, 88, 89
Morgan, A. W., 2, 6, 95
Mueller v. Allen, and tuition tax credits, 74, 75
Murphy, P. E., 6, 77-90

N

National Association of College Admissions Counselors (NACAC), 97
National Association of College and University Business Officers (NACUBO), 12, 94, 97
National Commission of Student Financial Assistance, 69, 72, 75
National Commission on the Financing of Postsecondary Education, 95
National Defense Education Act of 1958, 64
National Direct Student Loans, 65
National Institute of Education, 69
National Longitudinal Study, 69
Nerlove, M., 94, 95, 98
Neuberger, E., 96
New York, student aid in, 64
Northwestern University, loan capital for, 66

O

Objectives, optimization of, 25-27
Office of Management and Budget Circular A-21, 9, 38
Olson, J., 84, 89
O'Neill, J., 31, 34, 95
O'Neill, J. P., 85, 88, 89, 96
Oregon, as comparison state, 54
Ostheimer, R. H., 19, 34

P

Parasuraman, A., 89
Parent Loans for Undergraduate Students (PLUS), 65, 67
Payers: complex set of, 4; proportion of costs from, 15
Peer pricing: concept of, 14, 17, 37; factors in, 43-44
Pell Grants, 65, 68, 69
Pennsylvania, University of: loans at, 17-18; pricing at, 7-9, 15-17
Petroshius, S. M., 84, 88, 89
Pindyck, R. S., 21, 27, 34
Political process, concepts fundamental to, 47-49
Power, concept of, 48
Price: analysis of role of, 1-5; base, 10, 13, 17; cash cost, 11-12, 13; defined, 78; dimensions of, 79-84; forces on, 36-38; nature of, 77-79; sticker, 10, 13, 17; trends in, 1-2; types of, 10-12, 13
Price discounting. *See* Discount prices
Price lining, and psychological pricing, 84-85

Pricing: analysis of perspectives on, 7-18; background on, 7-10, 35-36; case studies of, 52-54, 56-58; compared, in public and private sectors, 58-61; complex, 3-4; conclusions on, 17-18, 44, 61; cost-related policy for, 24, 28-31; and costs, 12, 14-15; definitions in, 80; differential, 38-39; dimensions of, 80; economic context for, 58; enrollment demand models for, 19-34; example of policies on, 15-17; externally-indexed, 14, 17, 37, 42-43; financial strategies for, 84-85; increased interest in, 2-3; issues in, 9-10; mandated, 14-15, 37; marketing view of, 77-90; multiple, 85; nonfinancial strategies in, 85-88; peer, 14, 17, 37, 43-44; policy issues in, 60-61; political aspects of, 47-62; political processes in, 60; prestige, 84; and priorities and planning, 35-45; in private sector, 49-54, 58-61; proportional cost, 12, 14, 37, 38-42; psychological, 84-85; in public sector, 54-61; reducing burden of, 63-75; research agenda in, 91-94; residual, 14, 17, 37; resources on, 94-97; value-added, 14, 17, 37

Princeton University: financial data for, 8; Fund for Pious Youth at, 63

Productivity, and externally-indexed pricing, 42-43

Products, classification of, 80-81

Proportional cost pricing: concept of, 12, 14, 37; factors in, 38-42

R

Rados, D. L., 95
Reagan administration, 52, 65-66, 68, 71, 73, 74
Research, price of, 36
Research Institute of America, 97
Residual pricing, concept of, 14, 17, 37
Risk: defined, 80; factors of, 83-84; pricing, strategies for, 86, 87-88
Rochester, University of, medical school prices at, 15
Rockefeller, J. D., Jr., 9
Rubinfeld, D. L., 21, 27, 34
Rush Medical College, loan capital for, 66
Rusk, J. J., 61, 95

S

Schiffman, L. G., 80n, 89
Shaman, S., 5, 7-18, 37, 92
Sherman, D. G., 25-26, 33
Simon, H. A., 47, 61
Slosson, E. E., 7, 8n, 9, 18
Social Security, 65
Staffing, and enrollment demand model, 31
Stampen, J., 95
Stanford University: financial data for, 8; medical school prices at, 15
State Board for Community College Education, 56
Sticker price: concept of, 10, 13; trends in, 17
Stigler, G. J., 94
Strauss, G., 52, 61
Student financial aid: accomplishments of, 69-70; analysis of, 64-73; beneficiaries of, 70-72; developments in, 65-67; forms of, 65, 72-73; history of, 64; issues in, 67-73; loans as, 72-73; need for, 68-69; need versus merit issue in, 71-72; sources of, 64-65
Sullivan, D., 96
Supplemental Educational Opportunity Grants, 65
Suttle, J. L., 5, 47-62, 95

T

Tax policy, as price discounting, 73-75
Tierney, M. L., 11, 18, 85, 89
Time pricing: and marketing, 81-82; strategies for, 85-87
Tonn, J. C., 47, 61
Tuition: changes, responses to, 24-25; cost-related policy for, 28-31; and enrollment demand model, 23-25; setting, 23-24; subsidy, equation for, 26

U

Unbundling, and proportional cost pricing, 39-40, 85, 88
U.S. Army, 79

V

Value-added pricing, concept of, 14, 17, 37

Van Alstyne, C., 14, 18
Vanderbilt University, student loans from, 66
Veterans Readjustment Act, 64, 65
Viehland, D. W., 23, 24, 34
Virginia, University of, medical school prices at, 15
Vroom, V. H., 52, 61

W

Wabnick, R., 2, 6
Wang, W. K. S., 40, 44-45, 96
Ward, B., 94
Warner, T., 5, 35-45
Washington, pricing in, 54-61
Washington State University, pricing for, 57n
Washington, University of, pricing for, 56-57n
Washington University: medical school prices at, 15; prepayment plan of, 66
Weathersby, G. B., 19, 33
Weiler, W. C., 5, 19-34
Weinschrott, D., 19, 34
Western Washington University, pricing for, 57n
Wilson, F. S., 32, 34
Wilson, R. F., 39, 45, 94, 97, 98
Wing, P., 23, 34
Wisconsin, as comparison state, 54
Wisconsin-Whitewater, University of, shopping product of, 81
Wise, D. A., 27, 34, 69, 75, 96

Y

Yale University: financial data for, 8; pricing by, 49-54, 58-61
Yanikoski, R. A., 39, 45, 94, 97, 98

Z

Zemsky, R. M., 5, 7-18, 37, 92
Ziemthaml, V. A., 78, 87, 89

Ministry of Education & Training
MET Library
13th Floor, Mowat Block, Queen's Park
Toronto M7A 1L2